Early praise for Taigan

"If you have a desire to r̲e̲ [...]
rather for the intent to ch[...]   ın
lives her life with openne [...]
your own journey and examine your own convictions and [...]

— Rachelle Boschman

"I have read every single thing Taigan has blogged and put out and she writes so beautifully from her heart with such raw emotion and vulnerability. You won't be disappointed in her book. Get for yourself and for a friend… you will be glad you did."

—Aaron F.

"If you are looking for another book on simple steps to a good Christian life, this is not the book for you. Taigan Bombay's writing is raw, real, and not the typical "Christian" material. She pushes the traditional boundaries. However, her faith and relationship with Jesus is genuine. Long time Christians will be challenged in their thinking. Seekers will be encouraged to give Jesus a chance. Everyone will be released to live authentically."

— Elaine King, District Administrator,
Pentecostal Assemblies of Canada, Saskatchewan District Inc.

"Reading Taigan's writing is an experience that always lifts the heart and soothes the soul. Taigan brings vulnerability, relatability with a large dose of hope, reassurance and peace. All of that with her perfectly sprinkled sense of humour. Her words reach down to the hidden, the parts you weren't sure you could face. Taigan shines a light to show you're not alone and makes the ordinary not only enough but how it's in the ordinary that magic appears. Taigan's writing is brave and it makes me brave."

—Megan Harrison

"I found Taigan's blog from a friend years ago and her ability to be honest, real, and open was what drew me in and kept me coming back! I have always felt drawn to her posts, her words were exactly what I needed to be reading at that exact moment! I'm so proud of her for sharing your struggles and fears and reminding us that we are always enough! Her words truly are a gift and I've been blessed so many times over by reading each and every word she has shared and poured out."

— Kim Mogdan

TAIGAN BOMBAY

Selah
MOMENTS

THE EVERYDAY PLACES
WHERE I FIND GOD

Copyright © 2022 by Taigan Bombay and Alanna Rusnak Publishing

All rights reserved. This book or any portion thereof may not be reproduced or used in any manner whatsoever without the express written permission of the publisher except for the use of brief quotations in a book review or scholarly journal.

The information contained within this document is for educational and entertainment purposes only. This publication is not intended as a substitute for the advice of mental health or religious professionals.

Under no circumstance will any blame or legal responsibility be held against the publisher or author for any damages, reparation, or monetary loss due to the information contained within this book, either directly or indirectly.

First Printing: 2022
ALANNA RUSNAK PUBLISHING
ISBN: 978-1-990336-17-1

Alanna Rusnak Publishing
282906 Normanby/Bentinck Townline
Durham, Ontario, Canada, N0G 1R0

"Awesome God" Rich Mullins (1988) CCLI 41099; "As The Deer" Marty Nystrom (1984) CCLI 1431; "Raise A Hallelujah" Bethel Music CCLI 7119315; "Goodness of God" Bethel Music CCLI 7117726

"TSN Turning Point" © The Sports Network

"An Apple A Day" Lauren Talley, Kidsongs, Album #11292130

Scripture quotations taken from:

The Amplified® Bible (AMP), Copyright © 2015 by The Lockman Foundation. Used by permission. www.lockman.org; THE MESSAGE, copyright © 1993, 2002, 2018 by Eugene H. Peterson. Used by permission of NavPress. All rights reserved. Represented by Tyndale House Publishers, Inc.; THE HOLY BIBLE, NEW INTERNATIONAL VERSION®, NIV® Copyright © 1973, 1978, 1984, 2011 by Biblica, Inc.® Used by permission. All rights reserved worldwide; The Living Bible copyright © 1971 by Tyndale House Foundation. Used by permission of Tyndale House Publishers Inc., Carol Stream, Illinois 60188. All rights reserved. The Living Bible, TLB, and the The Living Bible logo are registered trademarks of Tyndale House Publishers; The Passion Translation®. Copyright © 2017, 2018, 2020 by Passion & Fire Ministries, Inc. Used by permission. All rights reserved. ThePassionTranslation.com; The Voice Bible Copyright © 2012 Thomas Nelson, Inc. The Voice™ translation © 2012 Ecclesia Bible Society All rights reserved.

Author photograph by Hillary Stratton of Stratton Creative Co.

Contact publisher for Library and Archives catalogue information.
Alanna Rusnak Publishing is an imprint of Chicken House Press
chickenhousepress.ca

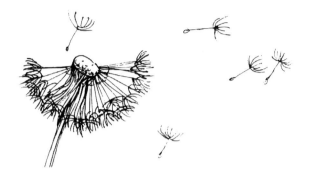

For my grandma, Marilyn. You have lived your life as an example for Jesus better than any sermon could ever preach. I am who I am because of you. I love you.

For Bennett. You are my joy. I found God when He gave me you. I love you.

Preface

The lie of your life will be that you are too far gone, too much, not enough, incapable, too late, too old, missed your opportunity, need to wait it out... and the list goes on!

Most of us will hinder ourselves from becoming the most current version of who we are are meant to be because we still associate ourselves with an earlier draft.

You can go through a rough season and still prevail.
You can fail and still succeed.
You can change your opinions and that doesn't mean you are a hypocrite.
You can move forward without shame, knowing that He is working out all things for good. Even the things you wish never happened.

All of it is part of our story and He uses it all to create the best, and final, draft.

Let go of the things you can't change and hang on to the things that they taught you.

If nobody has ever said this to you before, you need to know this: He's not holding anything over your head; He's bowed low, washing your feet.

Yes, even with everything He knows about you.

Keep moving forward. Keep writing the story of your life. Refuse to paralyzed by regret.

Your story is beautiful and it's not finished yet!

Contents

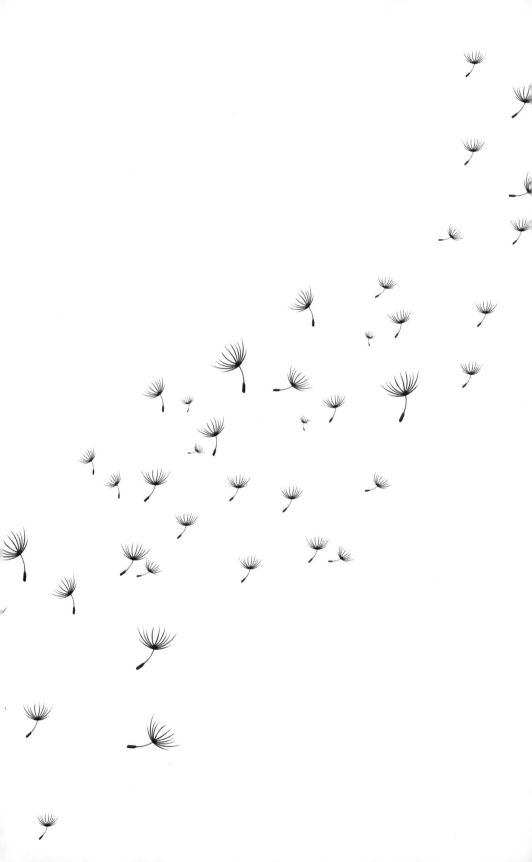

SELAH MOMENTS

The everyday places where I find God

TAIGAN BOMBAY

2022

1

Selah Moments

It's not always in a loud audible voice booming from Heaven;
sometimes it is in the everyday moments where we find God.

Do you consider yourself to be a spiritual person? Growing up, I wanted to be: always fascinated with the idea of God; mesmerized by wise and godly people. I remember being in junior high and praying that God would show up in my room so I could talk to Him.

I don't know if we all carry the same innate desire to know the most complex spiritual secrets. What I do know is that it has been the driving force of my walk with the Lord. It is the reason that I returned to Him when I still questioned everything. It is the reason why I refuse to let hard things break me. It is the reason I write. Period.

What makes a spiritual person spiritual? Is it a dedication to follow religious rules and standards? Is it giving money to the church? Is it praying until you fall asleep? Is it memorizing all the scripture? Those are practices that are acts of obedience to a larger commitment; however, as I get older, the more I recognize that those things are just the bones. There is still muscle, tissue, vessels, blood, tears, fat, and organs that surround the bones and fill in the spaces.

I would sit in church as a small child, overcome with excitement for the Lord. I am a person that feels. I am sensitive. I think a lot. I am constantly processing. Early in 2020, CBC News published an article claiming that some people lack an inner monologue. Who *are* those people? I am probably the way I am in order to bring balance to the world; I make up for their lack of inner dialogue by maintaining a constant conversation in my head.

Worship music moved me, especially at the Sunday night services. I remember the way my body and heart felt the first time I heard the chord progression to "As the Deer." Then there was that earth-shaking power ballad, "Awesome God." How many times did I want to jump up out of my pew, raise my hands, and see the Glory of the Lord fall in that place? Even at the tender age of 5.

The frequent narrative of my internal dialogue was this: "You're too young to be spiritual"—as if it was some sort of grown up sport. I was convinced that I had to be 50 years old to be close to God, and until that time arrived I could quietly enjoy those Sunday school felt board stories and terrifying puppets.

As a mother it has become very important to me that my children know it is okay to express themselves spiritually. I don't want them to grow up thinking they are too young to have deep God thoughts. I don't want them to believe they are too young to know the Lord in their own personal way. I don't want them to sit on the edge of their seat, apprehensively frozen while their whole body is longing to jump up and express externally what is happening internally. I don't want them to believe the lie that they need to have a mortgage, a couple of kids, local church membership, and a tithing number before they can be considered spiritual.

From the time my daughter was born, she was drawn to worship music. As an infant she would turn her head when we played worship videos on YouTube. She just wanted to catch a glimpse. When she reached the highchair stage, she would sit for hours watching her two favourite worship songs—"Raise A Hallelujah" and "Goodness of God"—over a heaping pile of grated marble cheese. (Sounds like heaven, doesn't it?) By the time she was a year old, she walked around with two arms straight up in the air yelling, "Heyyyy!" whenever we would say, "Praise the Lord!" And now, at the age of 2, she freely dances around our home with arms raised when we put any sort of worship music on.

If you ever needed to justify your early and innate desires to know God more deeply, look no further. You are not alone. Maybe you are still considered "young" and can identify with everything I have written so far. Maybe you are a little more "weathered" but you can still remember feeling and thinking some of the things I have shared.

We are never alone.

Here's what I have learned, and it applies at any age: *there is no qualifying age for your spiritual journey.*

He knew you and formed you in your mother's womb, which means your innate desire to be close to your Maker was there even before you were born.

Maybe you have lived a lot of years, and yet you still feel like you need permission to express yourself externally with what is happening internally.

Maybe you have never been told that you have a seat at the table.

Maybe you have been waiting a long time for your spiritual journey to begin.

Look no further.

You don't need permission.

It is your God-given right.

It is what you were made for.

So throw your hands up in the air.

You have always had a seat at the table. Come sit and eat.

You have been waiting to start a journey that you are already travelling on. Turn around and look. Do you see it?

The years, experiences, heartaches, victories, and seemingly meaningless moments? They're all there.

A number of years ago I became curious about this word 'selah.'

Even now it is a mystery to scholars and theologians. The word processing software I used to type this book does not even recognize it as a word.

Yet it is laced throughout scripture, often at the end of a song or poem. Through my research I have come to understand that the closest thing to a definition is this: *"pause and think on these things."*

It's a break in a song.

A pause after a deep thought.

A moment of quiet after something profound.

I live for the Selah moments of life: those quiet times when we stop and consider what has just occurred.

Journey with me through a hindsight perspective. Walk with me on my spiritual journey with the Lord.

It has not always been in the monumental moments, TSN turning points, or emotional highs.

It has been in the Selah moments—the every day moments—where I've found God.

Selah

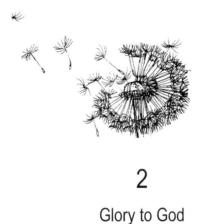

2

Glory to God

It's not always on the mountain top;
often it's in the valley where we find God.

During the holiday seasons, I usually find myself in a state of dread. I enjoy the relaxation; the hibernation; time with my kids; endless cups of coffee; daytime tv; trips to the mall; naps; quiet moments of reflection.

The dread may be rooted in seasonal exhaustion. Whatever it is, it leaves me feeling like I am missing the mark in my life.

"Is this it? Is this all?" I have asked.

Tired. Short. Irritated.

The Gen Y/Millennial in me wonders if I am successful enough. Will life ever be more than exhaustion, work, parenting, work, smatterings of victories, work, and always waiting for the future? You know… the future…when life falls magically into place?

If you are from my generation, you will know we have consistently been fed the narrative that we are all destined for greatness. We can be and do anything. Our lives are suppose to be Instagram-worthy, perfectly executed so we can get the "likes" that we deserve.

At this point I am a 36-year-old wife, mother, church planter, and dental hygienist with a creative streak.

Is it enough? I mean, if I were really living my best life would it have even an ounce of dread?

"Glory to glory," I heard the Lord whisper as He interjected my thoughts.

> *"And we all… are progressively being transformed into His image from one degree of glory to even more glory, which comes from the Lord, who is the Spirit."* 2 Corinthians 3:18

Our lives cannot exist solely on the mountain top.

In between the peaks of the mountains are the valleys. The spaces that keep us grounded and level before we get to the moments of glory and victory.

Sandwiched between the moments of glory is the "to."

The getting *to* that glory. It's the everyday life. The day to day stuff. The living and working and mom-ing. Yes, even the moments of exhaustion and feeling like it was just another day, but thank God we lived to see it.

For many years I would section my days, weeks, and months into blocks so I could look forward to something other than what was presently in front of me, always waiting for the moments of "when _____ finally happens."

The "to" paves long roads between glory moments.

Everyday responsibilities and regular life.

Mundane moments that remind us what the magnificent ones are.

It's all good. The everyday life. The mountain top moments. The successes. The failures. The admitting you are exhausted and over it. The wondering if any of it is enough.

It's all good.

> "*...And so we are transfigured much like the Messiah, our lives gradually becoming brighter and more beautiful as God enters our lives and we become like him.*" 2 Corinthians 3:18

Our lives are a success when we become more like Him.

Our lives become brighter and beautiful as we realize they are not made better by acquiring or doing more. They do not become brighter when they finally become easier. They are not beautiful because of what we do or have. They are not worthy based on how many people see it or affirm it.

They become brighter and more beautiful as we become more like Him.

On the mountain top and in the valley.

In the moments of glory and in the journey in between.

I pray that no matter what you face, you find Christ in the coming and the going.

I pray that you find Him in the moments of "to" sandwiched between the glory.

He is there. Shining brightly to make us and our lives more and more beautiful, until we become more like Him.

Selah

3

Better Than You Found Them

*It's not in our encounters with people of prominence; it is
in our interactions with everyday people where we find God.*

I often think about what it would be like to meet my heroes.

What would be like to interact with them? Would their on-stage persona translate to real life? Would I be welcome to talk to them and share with them how their preaching or music changed my life? Would they brush me off like I am a commoner? Would who they are on that platform translate into anything other than grace and kindness when they step off of it? Are they nice to everyone, or to just those within their inner circle?

As I was running through that thought process, I felt in my spirit what it would feel like to be brushed off by those people. I felt what it would be like to finally meet them, only to have them come across as miserable or too good. I felt what it would be like to get the impression that I was bothering them with my story, presence, or gratitude.

I remember thinking that they surely wouldn't behave like that. They are Christian leaders after all. I would expect them to be so gracious and kind.

In that moment I experienced a birds-eye view of myself and I saw what it would be like to interact with someone like me.

I am the furthest thing from a prominent Christian celebrity. I do not have a bright platform or a large following of people. Most of the congregants in our previous places of ministry did not even know my name or that I was married to a pastor on staff.

It alerted my heart to what it would be like to interact with me, whether you were a friend or a stranger.

What if they met me and found out I was a Christian?

What taste would that experience leave in their mouth?"

Would they feel like cared for? Heard? Loved? Wanted?

Would they know that they are just as worthy as the people within my closest circle?

These are the questions that call us to look inward.

These are the questions that allow us to leave people better than how we found them.

These are the questions that remind us of that good old Golden Rule: treat others the way you want to be treated.

How would you want to be affected by the people you admire the most?

I am sure one positive interaction with any of my heroes in the faith would leave me marked and changed forever.

Maybe you do not consider yourself a leader. Perhaps you would never use the words "hero of the faith" to describe yourself. Maybe there has not been any opportunity for you to mentor someone.

Here's what you need to know: ***there are always people watching your example and looking up to you.***

We all have our sphere of influence; whether you know it or not, you are constantly leaving people either better or worse than you found them.

It's time to start behaving as though you believe what you say you believe.

How do you leave the people that are influenced by YOU? Hopefully it's better than how you found them.

Selah

4

An Apple a Day

It's not on brightly lit platforms in grandiose stadiums; sometimes it is on brown carpeted stages in small town churches where we find God.

My first experience with platform ministry was at 7 years old. Up until that point I had only been a spectator, observing those wise beyond my years lead, teach, guide, and most importantly...perform on stage.

Like any good 80s or 90s kid I had a large collection of Christian cassettes. Long before Hillsong or any of their cute music tailored towards children, there were a lot of cringe-worthy options available. When I was about 5 years old my grandparents returned home from a gospel concert, and with them, my first Lauren Talley cassette.

I spent hours and hours listening to that tape. They were all in my singing range, the little girl was relatable, and most importantly they came with an instrumental version of all the songs which we called the "split tracks" on the B side of the cassette. (If you are too young to understand that... Google it!)

The joy of my life at the ripe old age of 7 was putting that tape in my cassette player, using my hair brush as a microphone, and singing to myself in the mirror. I wanted to be famous and I wanted to sing in front of people. I was convinced it was my calling in life and that one day I would be renowned.

My time to shine eventually arrived with the opportunity to sing for "gospel night" at my local church: a fancy title for church talent show.

I will never forget that day. I was so nervous that I felt sick to my stomach. *What if I forgot the words? What if I didn't start on time? What if I didn't start in the right key?*

The anxiety level I experienced that day was so high, I am surprised I committed to another singing opportunity ever again.

This was my first lesson in comfort zones and what it meant to push myself beyond my anxiety to do what I felt called to do.

Fear will always provide opportunities for a way out, but the Lord is constantly giving us opportunities to say no to fear, and push us beyond our anxiety into freedom.

Every time you say no to fear and conquer the thing that is causing your anxiety... you win.

I often wonder who I would be today and what limitations I would have put on my life if I hadn't pushed through my anxiety that day. What opportunities would I have walked away from over my lifetime had I not stood up from that orange pew and walked up to that platform with shaking knees when they called my name?

I remember standing on the stage and staring back at what felt like a sea of people. Have you ever participated in any situation that involves you staring face to face with a large crowd? I know some of you have not, because the lack of encouragement on your faces as spectators tells me so!

With trembling hands I gripped that old, sponge covered, bacteria infested microphone. The music kicked in and as I waited for my cue the voice of a woman in my church reared its head as I remembered her "suggestion" for my performance: *"You should do some actions when you sing…"*

Actions?! I hadn't considered that.

Within seconds her words added another dimension to my anxiety: *"Should I have thought about this earlier? Do I need them? Will everyone be wondering why I didn't do actions if I don't?"*

Even now, the spiral I experienced as a 7-year-old is painful to remember. I have always been pretty quick on my feet, so I thought: *Why not?! I can do actions. I was born for this.* *Insert jazz hands here*

The first note of my song kicked in and I panicked to gather enough saliva so I could swallow. It felt like I had a lump the size of a grapefruit in my throat and I remember thinking: *What if I can't swallow or breathe in time? What if I miss the start of the song?!*

I mustered up the strength to clear my throat and as my note approached, I began to sing:

> *"If an apple a day can keep a doctor away, think what a prayer could do!"*

The music was jazzy and Lauren's words and tone had a Southern drawl so I was definitely going to mimic that to the best of my ability. I don't remember my infamous actions from that day, but I do remember trying to create and execute them, all while holding a microphone. I am sure it was a disaster; but kids are quirky and adults are smitten with them.

If you have ever performed in public you know this: the first few minutes can be excruciating, especially when you are inexperienced; however, something happens the longer you stay up there: it gets easier. I remember that feeling almost twenty-eight years later. As I got into my groove of singing, it got less scary. I found my comfort zone. My feelings of anxiety turned into adrenaline.

This was the fight or flight response taking full effect and by the end of that song, my body had experienced a surge of energy that left me feeling high.

I learned so many things that day as I apprehensively approached the church stage.

The first was that *the call of God is rarely comfortable.* Did I know what the future had in store when I got up on the stage that day? No. However, when I look back with a hindsight perspective I can see the hand of the Lord preparing even through moments of discomfort, at an early age.

The second lesson I learned that day was this: *It is possible to push beyond those feelings of discomfort.* I had no idea that over the years I was going to encounter many opportunities to do things that I felt called to and most of the time, I would have to do them with a degree of discomfort.

I was unaware that one day I was going to marry a pastor, and by proxy I would have to be involved in things that made me feel anxious and unqualified. I was unaware that one day I would become a dental hygienist and battle anxiety every day before work for years before it stopped. I was unaware that my obedience at 7 was preparing me for opportunities to be obedient at 37.

As I nervously clutched the microphone that day, I learned that the Lord was graciously teaching me something that many people go a lifetime without learning: ***I am capable of overcoming hard things.***

What would my life have looked like if I backed out and didn't get up on the stage that day? What if I had left the church building and declared that I wasn't going to do it? What would I have taught myself if I had decided to become paralyzed by my fear, taking the easier route?

I didn't just walk away with an inflated ego that day. Sure, the handclaps and praises were great; having people come up to me and tell me I was a great singer was exhilarating; being asked to get up and do it again was flattering. The greatest reward, however, was walking off that stage and knowing that I could experience fear and turn it into freedom.

Our history with God is the most valuable asset to our future selves. It reminds us of what is possible by reminding us of what we have overcome. It mobilizes us when we become paralyzed with fear. It strengthens us when our knees become weak. It steadies us when our bodies begin to tremble.

We often define our turning point moments with the Lord as pendulum swings from achievement to loss; however, I want to suggest that our monumental moments are found in the seemingly small victories.

I hadn't thought about that moment in 1992 for a very long time until recently. When the Lord reminded me of it, He also revealed His guiding hand throughout that entire five-minute performance as I rose to local church fame.

He was there the entire time, preparing a solid foundation through the obedience of a 7-year-old and it brought with it a lifetime of opportunities to say "yes" when He calls.

It not always through parted skies and audible voices. Sometimes it's the 80s styled stages and old bacteria-filled microphones where we find God.

5

Love Over Fear

It's not always the moments of comfort and safety; sometimes it is in the depths of our greatest fears where we find God.

It has become customary for me to pray and ask the Lord for direction over the new year. Every year I choose a word I feel the Lord is impressing on my heart, spending the next 365 days making it my focus.

The first time I ever did this, I immediately felt like I was suppose to choose the word 'love' for my theme of the year.

There was no way it was my own idea because I avoid the word love at all costs.

I don't like it.

I don't like the way it is romanticized.

And, if I were being honest, it makes me uncomfortable.

As much as I would have liked to wait for a better word to surface in my heart, I knew that I was being prompted by the Lord to push through and embrace the word 'love' for 2017.

At first I thought this journey would be about learning to love others because it's an area I struggle with. However, as time progressed it became increasingly clear I was going to be embarking on a journey that would involve *self*-love.

Quickly I began to embrace this simple truth: you can't love others if you don't love yourself.

It was a few months into 2017—the year of love—when an online baptismal service caused me to reflect on the time I was baptized at the age of 14. I watched the participants enjoy their moment and I noticed that their baptism was full of life, excitement, and celebration. This was not something I typically associated with baptisms. Growing up they were somber, serious, and ceremonial. It was a task to complete rather than a reason to celebrate. In that moment, I said out loud to myself: "I need a baptismal do-over. My first baptism was completely based out of fear."

Fear of letting people down.

Fear of being labelled a sinner.

Fear of going to hell.

My only reason for being baptized at 14 was that I thought I had to do it to get into Heaven. I was uneducated, misinformed, and completely driven by fear when it came to my relationship with God.

As I started thinking about this one moment in my life, it was like my mind started flipping through a Rolodex of time and it showed me how much of my life was, and still is, lived out of fear.

When fear creeps into your life, it becomes a disease that takes over your entire being.

It had infiltrated every aspect of my adult life; I didn't even realize that it wasn't normal or healthy. When I finally had the revelation of how I had been living, all I could think was: *"Really? I let THAT control me all of this time?"*

It has controlled my relationships, parenting, mental health, career, self-image, eating habits, finances, decision making, friendships, ministry life, ideas about God, and the list goes on. Honestly, just name an area of life and it was controlled by fear.

Then the Lord, in all His grace and mercy, reminded me of 1 John 4:18:

"there is no fear in love, perfect love casts out fear."

I had read that verse many times before, but this time, my spiritual eyes and ears widened. This time was the first time that I truly heard what it was saying.

I began to see why the Lord had asked me to direct 2017 towards this word 'love.'

Complete love gets rid of fear because there is no room for it.

When you find out what love really means and who He really is, it will start to break the chains that hold you down. It will release you. You will finally be free to be who you were created to be.

God is love.

He is perfect love, and His love casts our fear aside.

Understanding this will change the lens through which you view your entire life.

Fear says you need to jump through hoops to prove yourself.
Love says you are worthy where you stand.

Fear says you will never have a future.
Love says that you have a future and a hope.

Fear says that you will always go without.
Love says that He is more than enough.

Fear says that you are unlovable and second best.
Love says that you were bought with a price and His first choice.

Fear says that your problems are too big to be solved.
Love says that He's already got a solution.

Fear says that you are an outcast, only worthy of watching from the sidelines.
Love says that it is what qualifies you and wraps you in favour.

> *"There is no fear in love, but perfect love casts out fear. For fear has to do with punishment, and whoever fears has not been perfected by love."* 1 John 4:18

Shortly after this revelation, I felt the Lord nudging me to get baptized again. A baptismal do-over.

When my husband baptized me in water I wasn't afraid; I was free. I finally understood why others found reason to celebrate as they rose from the water. As I moved forward from that moment I was starting with a new foundation. This time, it was anchored in love. A firm foundation. Not rooted in fear, but built on the knowledge of His love for me (and you).

From this foundation we build.

We build to heights higher than we could have ever imagined, and we do it with confidence, harnessed in the safety and shelter of the Most High.

Selah

6

Pulling Weeds

It's not always in beautifully manicured gardens and fully bloomed flowers; sometimes it is in the weeds where we find God.

"I, God, search the heart and examine the mind. I get to the heart of the human. I get to the root of things. I treat them as they really are, not as they pretend to be." Jeremiah 17:9

I used to read this verse from the perspective of *He doesn't judge like the world does*; or, *beauty is on the inside. That's what God looks for. He knows my heart.*

I have started to see this verse differently as I feel the Lord pulling out the weeds and cleaning up the soil bed of my heart, getting to where the root of things are.

It hurts. And I feel like He is taking out more than He is leaving behind, as if there is nothing 'good' left to show for all of the years of gardening.

But that's the things about weeds.

They infiltrate an entire soil bed if they aren't properly tended to. They take over. They can eventually fill in the spaces where all the good things want to grow. Sometimes they even disguise themselves as flowers. Ugly flowers. Not the ones you want to keep around for long because once they are removed from their root system, they wilt and die immediately.

Just as a gardener treats them like they really are (and not as they pretend to be) God puts His hand on those weeds that are trying to be flowers and begins to rip them out. One by one.

If you've ever witnessed the aftermath of a pruning, you know that at first it looks bare. Exposed. Empty. You wonder what good will ever come out of it.

But that's the beauty. When we feel like we are taking steps backwards, usually we are getting closer to where we truly want to be.

Healthy. Flourishing. Alive.

The place where we can feel God pulling out the weeds and getting to the root of our hearts is actually just a sign that we have allowed a gardener to come into our flowerbeds, coaxing us back to a place of health.

It hurts.
It sucks.
It takes work.

Vulnerability and exposure in these areas is never comfortable, but it is necessary.

When you feel like God is pulling on your heart, uprooting you, know that He's actually preparing you.

He's keeping you healthy.
He's making room for you to flourish.
He's getting to the root of things.

He is treating and tending to things as they really are and not as they pretend to be.

All so that we can become who we are suppose to be.

Selah

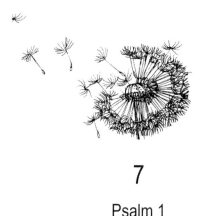

7

Psalm 1

*It's not always in seminary or institutes of higher education;
sometimes it is in Sunday School where we find God.*

My earliest memory of scripture is Psalm Chapter 1. It was the first passage I memorized after John 3:16. It feels like just yesterday that I sat at a round wooden table in my church Sunday school classroom, reciting each word for my friends and leaders.

Growing up I generally attended church with my grandparents. My grandma was the church secretary, and my grandpa a devoted usher. I remember being there whenever the doors were open, which included Wednesday night Pioneer Clubs, early Sunday morning "Sunday School," and of course, children's church which took place during the regular church service.

I'll never forget the year I arrived at my early morning Sunday school class and discovered I had the best teacher ever that year! Martha, a young leader, was one of those people I wanted to be just like when I grew up.

As our class started, we were told our curriculum for that season would be Psalm Chapter 1. Each week we were going to add a new line of the passage to our memory bank and discuss what the sentence meant.

What about the felt boards?

What about games?

What about the video lessons?

They were all a distant memory. This was the big leagues. We weren't babies anymore. It was time to start learning scripture and planting some biblical roots in our souls.

To this day, more than twenty-five years later, I can still recite that chapter without missing a beat. Do you know it?

> *"Blessed is the man*
> *Who walks not in the counsel of the ungodly,*
> *Nor stands in the path of sinners,*
> *Nor sits in the seat of the scornful;*
> *But his delight is in the law of the Lord,*
> *And in His law he meditates day and night.*
> *He shall be like a tree*
> *Planted by the rivers of water,*
> *That brings forth its fruit in its season,*
> *Whose leaf also shall not wither;*
> *And whatever he does shall prosper.*
> *The ungodly are not so,*
> *But are like the chaff which the wind drives away.*
> *Therefore the ungodly shall not stand in the judgment,*
> *Nor sinners in the congregation of the righteous.*

For the Lord knows the way of the righteous,
But the way of the ungodly shall perish. "

At the age of 10, I had no idea what any of that meant. But there was one vision created by scripture that I consistently got hung upon: "He shall be like a tree planted by the rivers of water, that brings forth its fruit in its season."

I always envisioned a large tree, strong and steady, sitting on a bank as water rushed by. Green and colourful. Gently swaying in the wind. The calming sound of leaves rustling with each gust.

I was young and struggled with unpacking the meaning in the words I was memorizing; however, the seeds planted by reciting those words took root deep within my soul and they've had a lasting affect on my spiritual journey.

We can be so quick to disregard the beginning of a thing. Whether it's physical exercise or the first steps in our spiritual journey, we look to the future, praying that our desired outcome would unfold quickly.

There is no such thing as an overnight success.

When we make the decision to get in shape, we want to be fit... yesterday, yet it takes months of movement and discipline to see results. When we ask God to give us a glimpse of His infinite wisdom, we wonder why He couldn't just tell us everything now and make us wise in a moment; yet it takes years of planting seeds and developing roots, until one day we discover that we are that tree planted by the rivers, bearing fruit.

Whenever I find myself in a winter season of life, I always go back to Psalm 1. I can recite it to myself under my breath. I translate what the words are saying when I need to remember what true happiness is. "My joy is in following the word of the Lord, my joy is found in thinking about what He has said day and night. When I do that, I will be strong and healthy like a tree by a water source. I will see the fruit when the season is right."

I had no idea when I was 10 years old that my Sunday school memory verses would be the seeds to a sequoia. What began as a fragile, small, and immature faith, grew into a strong, developed, and deep history with God.

Don't disregard the beginning. Each step in our walk with the Lord is a seed being planted for a future harvest.

Selah

8

Party Time

It's not always in our ability to comfort others; often times it is in our ability to rejoice with them where we find God.

A number of years ago I had the joy and privilege of teaching my son about birthdays. One morning, as we were leaving the house for a birthday party, I explained to Bennett that it was his friend Gabe's birthday.

A look of pain and discomfort immediately washed over his face, and with a big meltdown he declared: *THAT IS NOT FAIR!*

Me: Why?
Bennett: Because it's suppose to be my birthday first.
Me: No, that's not now it works. Your birthday is next. In July.
Bennett: Well how old is he going to be?
Me: He is 6 today!

Bennett: WHAT? That is DEFINITELY NOT FAIR!
Me: Why?
Bennett: Because I want to be 6!
Me: That's not how it works. He was born before you. You have to be
*   5 before you can be 6.*

The lamenting continued as I tried to explain to my almost-5-year-old that he had to learn how to be happy for others and rejoice with them especially when it came to their birthdays.

Upon arrival, we opened the door and the newly 6-year-old jumped across the landing with a shiny new toy in tow: *"Hey, Bennett! Look at my new toy! It's my birthday! I got more presents, come and look!"*

My son stood on the landing, brows furrowed in rage, arms crossed, barely able to look Gabe in the eyes; and, with jealousy oozing from his body declared, *"They're terrible. Just awful."*

As a parent I was mortified. Baffled that *MY* child would behave in such a distasteful way, I tried to think of all the lessons I could teach him in that moment. Then I started to look inward and I realized that all of his emotions were familiar.

How often do we stand on the landing of life, look up at others rejoicing in their moment, thinking to ourselves: *That's terrible. Just awful.*

Truthfully, we all know it's not terrible or awful. We don't really believe that. We just wish it was ours. Our day. Our moment.

I have come leaps and bounds in my quest to be happy for others; however, there is still a part of me that struggles. Perhaps it is the lie that lingers and tells me: "You aren't worthy of what they have and God doesn't think you are worthy either."

We spend most of our days living regular lives. We are faithful, hard working, bill paying, adult-behaving, parents, friends, and leaders. When our "big day" comes (you know those big days, they are the ones that are better and brighter than all of those normal days) we want to rejoice; and we want others to rejoice along with us.

Our big moment.
Our blessing.
Our breakthrough.
Our new beginning.
Our celebration.

For our own benefit, and for the benefit of others, *we have to learn what it means to rejoice with those who rejoice.*

To decide that we are going to love so extravagantly that jealousy doesn't have a place in the room.

Get out the balloons.
Bring a gift that you would want to receive.
Eat a piece of cake even if you don't like the flavour.
Strap the blindfold on and take a swing at the piñata.
Sing "Happy Birthday" at the top of your lungs.
Clap when they blow out the candles.
Gather around with a smile as they open gifts.

This is love.

This is faithfulness.

This is growing up in God.

This is the security that comes in knowing that He loves us all, but that not every day is our birthday moment.

It is okay. In fact, it is good.

Your time will eventually come around, and when it does you will want people to get out all of the supplies and throw a party for you.

God help us to be people that love so genuinely that we can't help but rejoice for others, perhaps even before they realize they have a reason to rejoice.

Help us to be people that see life in days and moments, to not broad stroke your blessings and favour as all or nothing.

Help us to be reminded of the security and future found in You, and not the limitations we place on You.

He rejoices over each of us and He invites us to rejoice over others right along with Him.

Selah

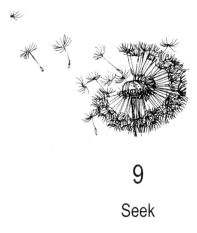

9

Seek

It's not always in the obvious;
sometimes it is in the seeking where we find God.

Many of us ask God to prove that He is real.

We need a sign. An answer. A divine encounter.

You name it, we've asked for it. Our faith and belief systems are hinged on the conditions that we place on Him. We think we need proof of His existence. I did this for most of my life.

A number of years ago, I asked God why some people stay where they are in their relationship with Him, and why others seem to progress and hear from Him more. Does He choose favourites? Does He predestine who can hear from Him? Are there some that are just better "set up" to know Him more?

Quietly He whispered:

> *"You will seek me, and find me. When you seek me with all your heart."* Jeremiah 29:13

The answer isn't performance or worth. It's not based on jumping through hoops. It's not determined by playing favourites, or even genetics.

It is in the seeking.

You will need to seek Him if you want to know Him.

In our drive-thru loving, quick-fix society, we have this idea that when we want something, we should immediately get it. Our ideas on this topic don't end when it comes to God.

"God, reveal yourself to me."
"God, why do you let bad things happen to good people?"
"God, why don't you fix this?"
"God, if you are real, you'll _____ for me."

We demand instead of seek.
We wait instead of work.
We talk instead of listen.

He's got a lot to say but He isn't a clanging symbol; He's a gentle whisper.

If you want to know Him.
If you want to hear Him.
If you want to see Him.
If you want to find Him.
… You will have to seek Him.

You'll have to pray, and listen.

You'll have to read, and digest.

You'll have to push through when it's hard.

You'll have to keep searching even when you don't want to.

You'll need to do all of that, with all of your heart.

And you will need to seek like your life depends on it.

Because it does.

It's not enough to just have proof that He is real. You need to desire to know Him because you can't live without Him.

All of His promises are yes and amen.

And this is the promise: *"You will find me."*

When?

When you seek Him with all of your heart.

There are no favourites. Just seekers that keep on searching until they find Him. Keep seeking.

When you do, you will find Him.

And when you do find Him, He's so big and obvious and visible, it's unlikely that you will ever need to ask for a sign again.

Selah

10

Bulletins

It's not always in the turning of Biblical pages;
sometimes it is in the folding of bulletins where we find God.

Growing up I spent most of my time at church with my grandma. She was the church secretary, and it felt as though if the doors were open, she was there. So that meant I was there. I loved hanging out with her in the church office. I liked when she would assign jobs, and I would do them with passion and perfection.

One of my favourite jobs was folding bulletins. There was something so exciting about folding those small tickets of information. Maybe it was because I had first exposure to the new week's wealth of information. Maybe it was because I loved the smell of the hot paper as it flew out of the copier in stacks. All I know is that I always said "yes" to the opportunity to fold bulletins; however, I can't lie: I loathed the weeks when there were inserts. So much extra work.

This was one my most frequent tasks for years until I got replaced by a fancy new photocopier that could do it for me. (My first taste of being replaced by technology.) My run was fairly long, considering I still remember folding those bulletins as a 12-year-old.

It was a random summer Friday when I found myself with my grandma, sitting in the air-conditioned office at our church. I remember it clearly. I worked away at my task, listening to the background chatter of constant information and unending church gossip. I was annoyed by all of it. Even at a young age I couldn't stand church politics. Whether it was the pastor's wife that told me I should wear more dresses to church (eye roll), or the drama over church music, I was pretty much done, and my life in ministry wasn't even near getting started.

As I folded (right end folded to the left, left side folded over the right), I blurted out, "Oh, good Lord! Who in their right mind would ever want to marry a pastor? I could never do it. I wouldn't want to spend my life being all... fake and stuff!"

My grandma's response still replays in my mind. With a look to the side, and smirk on her face, she calmly said, "Oh Taigan, you better be careful what you say. You just never know what could happen."

This is the part where I tell you that God has a sense of humour. It wasn't even ten years later that I found myself marrying the youth pastor that I met in that exact same spot, in that exact same church office.

The first time I heard about Matt was from my grandma one August afternoon:

"We are getting a new youth pastor! He's a Bombay!"

"What does that even mean, Grandma? Who cares..."

Perhaps that is why I find myself where I am today. I wasn't swayed by 'big names,' and church politics. I never cared about playing the church game, and I married a man that doesn't either. From a very young age I was nauseated by the way grown adults behaved in church. It seemed that most people wanted their own agenda fulfilled no matter the cost, disregarding God throughout the entire process.

Years later and about two years into ministry, I came face to face with the Lord in prayer, and said this out loud:

"I am going to spend the rest of my life in ministry being who I am, and I will never play a game to make people happy. I want to be the pastor's wife that I wish I had when I was young. Life is not perfect, and I'm not either. I will never pretend that I have it all together."

I didn't know then how uncomfortable that would make a lot of people. (Mostly other people in ministry.) It has been a double-edged sword; yet to this day, the benefit still outweighs the risk.

For every person that has been turned off, there have been two that have been set free. That math will always be worth it to me.

Over the years my technique has become more refined and my approach more mature, but my vision still remains the same: stay true to who God has called me to be and be a person of transparency.

I don't always get it right, and I know that my motives are not always one hundred percent pure. Yes, there is part of me that still loves to make people wiggle, and I still hate church politics. (Hence why we are church planters.) However, I have felt the hand of God on my life and the blessing of the Lord releasing me to be who He has called me to be.

Whenever I wonder if my husband deserved a more reverent and reserved partner in ministry, I hear God's whisper: *"You're exactly who He needed."*

Whenever I feel like it would be easier to just go along to get along and shut up when something doesn't sit right, I feel the prompting of the

Lord: *"That's not who I asked you to be."*

Whenever I start to question who I am or wonder if maybe I would be further along on the man-made ladder of Christian success if I could just keep my mouth shut, He quietly reminds me of the little girl folding bulletins in her grandma's office: *"You're doing just fine."*

Selah

11

The One in Front of You

*It's not always in the large masses sitting in the church pews;
it is often in the one that's in front of you where we find God.*

Sometimes we make something that is very simple so complicated.

For a long time I didn't think I was cut out for ministry. I didn't think I was patient enough, spiritual enough, well trained, or accepted. To distract from those things, I decided to be so 'real' that I separated myself.

We often believe the lie that we have to behave a certain way or adopt a belief system that predicts an outcome before it happens so we can say we were right. Before someone could tell me that I wasn't enough, I could say, "I already know. Here it is. Take it or leave it. And you'll probably decide to leave it once you get too close."

This is pride rearing its head. It builds walls around us so that we can say, "I'll just keep you over there before you can come over here and hurt me."

What God has been showing me is that regardless of training, life experience, or career choices, I am in ministry. And you are too.

We often hold that title for the people on platforms with credentials and titles. But the truth is, whether you are a dental hygienist or a construction worker, if you believe in Jesus you are in full time ministry.

Ministry isn't reserved for platforms or positions. It isn't for those who appear to be really good at leadership. It's not only for the most eloquent or the most educated theologians, it is for all of us.

If you have a relationship with God and you have chosen to follow Him, you have been called to ministry. And here is your job description: love the person that is standing in front of you at this very moment.

It is not complicated.

It's cups of coffee and lunch dates.
It's small conversations with big impact.
It's smiling at a stranger and patience with people that test it.
It's loving your kids and your spouse well.
It's contributing at your church and asking where you can help.
It's every day and every hour and with every person that is in front of you.

Sometimes it just starts with loving ourselves: the person in the mirror looking back at us.

Ministry is loving the person in front of you.

The one.
The lonely.

The hurting.
The sick.
The depressed.
The anxious.
The stressed out.

Ourselves.
Our family.
Our friends.
Our coworkers.
Our neighbours.
Our church family.

It's about getting closer to Him so that we leave the fragrance of Jesus wherever we go.

Little by little.

Encounter by encounter.

Time after time.

Day after day.

Moment by moment.

We often get it twisted. We think great ministries are large and meeting cultural expectations. It can be performance driven and for the masses but Jesus calls us to go after the one.

Ministry is loving the person in front of you.

If you have been asking God for a ministry, or call on your life, here it is:

Be present.
Live well.

Love the very one in front of you.
Here and now.

Selah

12

Perfect Love

*It's not found behind our high walls of protection
or guarded hearts; it is in our vulnerability and
willingness to love where we find God.*

When the Lord asked me to make the word 'love' my word, for the year 2017, I cringed.

It seemed so cliché. Everyone thinks that love will change the world, but it seems that the world is just getting worse.

I haven't really ever been a people person... I mean, I want to be, but sometimes it's all just too hard.

People are complicated. They can be unreasonable and selfish; and yet, as we have been told by our dear Mother Theresa: "Love them anyway."

The day I took the step of faith to get baptized again, it unlocked a whole new level of love in my life.

It's just like God to tell us where we have walked in fear and then, when we are obedient to His call, He rewards us with blessing.

After I got baptized I felt an instant shift in my heart. Not that perfection had been reached, but something within me changed from selfishness to the desire to love.

I began to ask God to show me ways that I could love people freely instead of asking them to love me for who I was before I could love them back.

I experienced something that showed me just how much the enemy had tried to keep me secluded, angry, jealous, extremely introverted, and skeptical.

The thing is, if the enemy can keep you from people, He will keep you from love. And he knows that love is the essence of the Christian life. It's our driving force, because God *is* love.

When we find love we find connection.
Significance.
Acceptance.
Belonging.
Family.

For years my inability to love myself has kept me from loving people. Always an excuse: they're annoying, critical, hard to get along with, selfish, self absorbed, needy, relentless. You name a trait, and I had it on a list of reasons why I couldn't make relationships work.

Out of fear of being burned first, I saturated all my bridges with kerosene and lit them on fire; and then, without remorse, I set up a chair, hunkered down, and watched them all burn.

Why?

I wanted to prove a point.
I was afraid of being hurt.
I thought I deserved more.
I had enough jealousy to fill an ocean.
I thought it seemed easier to be alone than deal with relationships.

I restricted myself to a small handful people because they were the only ones that could 'handle me.'

I danced with social media through highs and lows because it gave me the false belief that people are disposable, and if they make you angry, jealous, or irritated you can get rid of them at a moment's notice.

I sat at a distance and watched from the sidelines, believing that to be loved I had to fill a certain mold, one that I would never conform to.

It was all lies and tactics to keep me from the very thing I was created for:

Connection.
Relationship.
Belonging.
Friendship.
Love.

The Kingdom of God is upside down and backwards to our cultural norms.

To overflow, we must give.
To feel significant, we must lift others high.
To be a leader, we must bow low.
To find our purpose, we must call others into their own.

The more I learn, the more I realize that all the negative attributes we find in people are just opportunities to a fill a void that is aching for love.

Anger is the covering for sadness.

Annoying is the call to be heard.

Self promotion, the desire to be significant.

Strong overbearing opinions, the need to have a voice and keep control.

Any negative attribute can be picked through, until we get to the root, which was once just a seed that wanted to be loved.

When you grasp the overwhelming love God has for you, you begin to see His love for others too. It is so profound that you can't help but ask Him for tangible ways to love the people around you more.

His ways are practical and they are laced throughout scripture:

Treat others how you would want to be treated.

Go to people when you have offended them, and apologize.

Keep forgiving over and over.

Feed them. It doesn't have to be fancy.

Wash feet and serve them well.

The Lord opened my eyes to the amazing people and opportunities for relationship that I have. I have never been more repentant and remorseful than when He showed me how I had distanced myself.

How I blocked the stream of love from flowing into my life and out to others.

How I reduced people to inconveniences and disruptions to my peace.

How I believed that others were disposable and replaceable, all in one.

I used to think that when He worked all things out for my good, it would be in a way that makes me comfortable, happy, and selfishly fulfilled. Now I am seeing that His idea of good is better than mine.

He takes fear and works it into love.

Seclusion is turned into community.

Bitterness into joy.
Dysfunction into family.

He takes burned bridges and He gives us the tools to repair, rebuild, and reconnect. He gives us a blueprint for a good, solid foundation and it is built on love.

Selah

13

It Matters

*It's not in our ability to perfect our talent; it is in
our willingness to show up where we find God.*

S omeone once told me that they went back to church because of my
writing.

I don't say that to toot my own horn or to make myself sound impressive
but to tell you that whatever you are putting your heart and soul into: it
matters.

The coming and going, the ins and the outs, the day after day, the
   faithfulness to your call: it matters.
The sweaty palms and racing heart when you step into something you
   feel called to: it matters.
The thing that looks like it may be insignificant or unoriginal: it matters.
The traits and talents that you question: they matters.

The things you wonder whether anyone notices: they matter.
The hobby that you love: it matters.

It matters because He is notorious for leaving the crowd and going after the one.

Whether you ever reach success by the world's standards, or you simply reach one person, you are successful.

Whether I ever have a bestselling book, or I just keep putting my heart out in blog posts: it still matters.

When your call is clear, success is inevitable.

My call is to point everything back to Him.

The ups and downs, the moments of pain, the joys, and (of course) the things that surprise people. They all matter, and how I share them with the world matters, because He is in all of it.

The goal isn't to get people to follow rules, act better, or behave themselves. It is to point to Him, because when we see Him, all of that other stuff moves to the sidelines.

The goal is to turn others to Him, so they too can step into their calling and purpose.

To find love and share love.
To move away from fear and into freedom.
To taste and see that the Lord is good.

Your failed attempts and moments of glory.
Your insecurities and your confidences.
Your fears and your unshakeable faith.

Your story

Your call.
Your life.

It all matters.
Because it all points back to Him.

And that is what truly matters.

Selah

14

Bitterness

It's not always in prophetic words at the altar; sometimes it is in the reactionary words of a 12-year-old where we find God.

When I was in seventh grade one of my childhood friends told me I was bitter and angry.

This shocked me because I had never been called that before, let alone considered that it was part of my personality. I always thought myself to be fun and silly—maybe a bit insecure, but never angry or harsh. If anything, I just wanted to be cool.

Somewhat hurt and a little annoyed, I remember thinking that it must be true if they felt the need to call it out in me, and over time it became how I labelled myself.

After a while, it wasn't just a passing comment; it became part of my identity, and whenever I tried to think of something good about myself, I would always go back to, "Yeah, but I'm still just bitter and angry. What good could come of that? It's all over me."

You're probably thinking, *"Wow. She really holds on to things."* And yes, I do. You should try being married to me.

I still catch myself wondering if I will ever have the label of bitter and angry removed from me and I feel convinced that's how everyone sees me.

What you dwell on you will become. What was once a passing comment from a kid (that didn't even know who *they* were, let alone who I was) eventually became part of my identity.

"As a man thinks in their heart, so is he." Proverbs 23:7

I have heard the Lord prompt me time and time again to ask Him this question: "Who do *you* say I am?"

"Who do you say I am, Lord?"

When Jesus asked the disciples this question in Matthew, he blessed them when they responded with truth and not with what they had heard from others about Him.

We need to go back to this practice time and time again. Because opinions are not truth. We like to label people. We like to categorize attitudes, issues, problems, and people. However, when we do this we stop looking at the person, and we focus solely on the one aspect that is merely a small facet of their personality.

"Who do you say I am, Lord?"

Listen for an answer. You will hear it if you are listening. You'll know it's Him if it points to the goodness of His design. If it reminds you that you are His. If you are encouraged.

Those whispers don't lie. They scream truth.

If you ask and all you hear is negatives or those things that you are lacking... go back. Wait. Listen again. Listen beyond your internal critic and the well meaning, sometimes unauthorized, voices around you.

When you hear who He says you are, it changes everything. It takes you back to the place of simply being a child of God, not a hot mess of an adult that can never get it right.

"Who do you say I am, Lord?"

Worthy.
Daughter.
Loved.
Happy.
Blessed.
Justified.
Fruitful.
Set apart.
Radiant.

Ask Him and listen for the things that you hear in your spirit. Nobody can ever take that from you or replace them.

Are we perfect? No. But the areas of imperfection are just places where He is still working things out for our good. He knows who we are and who we are becoming.

"Who do you say I am, Lord?"

When we meet with Him face to face and wait as He answers, His light shines on us; not only do we begin to become who we were meant to be, we radiate because we've seen Him in the process.

That is how we bring light to who we really are and not just who we have believed ourselves to be.

Wait.
Listen.
Be still.
Know the truth.
That is what will set you free to be who you truly are.

Selah

15

Baptize Me

*It's not always in religious practices and carefully
kept rules; sometimes it is in the second chances
and do-overs of life where we find God.*

When I was 14, I decided to check the last remaining thing off of my Christian to-do list, and I got baptized.

Up until this point, I had done all the right things: I had been dedicated to the Lord by my parents in front of our church; I had "asked Jesus into my heart" at 5 years old; I attended weekly Sunday school classes; I showed up on Wednesday nights for the mid-week kid's program; I participated in all the kid's choir stuff. The list goes on.

There was one thing that haunted me in the back of my mind: "Eventually I am going to have to go up there and get dunked in front of all those people…"

The thought crippled me. I had learned to tackle the stage when it came to singing, but speaking? No. There was no way. I wasn't doing it.

I struggled with these thoughts for a number of years and I considered all the ways I could get out of being baptized. Most of them related to waiting until I was older and more comfortable talking in front of people. Eventually, the fear of going to hell if I didn't get up there and get dunked got the better of me and I signed myself up.

At 36, when I think about the torment I went through at14, it breaks my heart. There was no education or teaching on why this was a practice that we did in our churches. There was no understanding on the history of baptism. There was only fear.

I don't remember my baptism. I have always been good with the details of my life, but this is a memory I truly don't have. Perhaps because I was so paralyzed by fear.

All I remember was the relief I experienced having finally 'got that over with.'

It's no surprise that God let me off that easy because many years later, at the age of 32, I felt the Lord prompting me to have a baptism do-over.

> *"That's what baptism into the life of Jesus means. When we are lowered into the water, it is like the burial of Jesus; when we are raised up out of the water, it is like the resurrection of Jesus. Each of us is raised into a light-filled world by our Father so that we can see where we're going in our new grace-sovereign country."* Romans 6:4-5

It wasn't until I was married and many years into ministry, that I learned what baptism was actually about. It's not a checkmark on the Christian to-do list of life; it's not something to get through to avoid hell; and it's not a fast pass to Heaven.

No, baptism in water is so much more exciting than that. It's the external declaration of an internal change. It's cleansing. It's resurrection after the death of self so we can experience life through Him. It's the first exposure to the Light after a very dark night.

I remember watching people being baptized online one evening and seeing the joy of Lord all over them as they jumped up out of the water and finally felt free. The great reset. A do-over after what may have felt like a lifetime of failures. As I sat there watching with a smirk on my face, I heard the whisper of the Lord: *"I want you to get baptized again, but this time because of your faith not your fear."*

I had experienced so much. I had come out of a season of darkness and it felt as though the Lord was awakening me to all of the lost and broken things that still needed attention.

"Ugh, but what would people think? A pastor's wife at a large church? Getting baptized? I'm sure people will think that I should have got this over with years ago. How can I now?"

The excuses circled around my head for a week until I finally couldn't handle the burden of His call anymore. If anything, through this experience I learned that when I made my pact with God to be real, it meant everything. Even the things that make me embarrassed and uncomfortable. Even the things that feel out of my control. Even the things that feel below the standard of spiritual maturity that I have set for myself.

On Mother's Day of 2017, I had my baptism do-over, one of the great memories of joy in my life. My husband baptized me, and in my pre-recorded video of why I chose to be baptized, I was able to speak to the spirit of fear that haunts so many of our lives. Something broke in my life that day, and as I walked away from that baptism tank, I carried a new joy in the Lord. I felt free. I felt renewed. I didn't know it yet, but I had unlocked a new level of faith in my life.

That decision to say "yes" and to be obedient to the prompting of the Lord, set in motion promises and dreams that I am living today. Most of my life had been lived in fear, and I recognized it. That day, when I stood in front of a thousand people and said, "I have lived a life of fear, but the Lord says to be anxious and afraid for nothing, so I choose to be free…" the spirit of fear broke away from my life and chronic anxiety became a memory.

Sometimes God asks us to do things that make us feel crazy, not because He's trying to make us look stupid, but because He's trying to set us free.

Selah

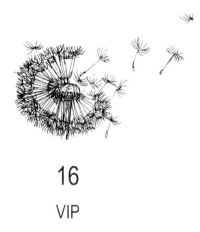

16

VIP

*It's not always in the calm moments of spiritual maturity;
sometimes it is in our fits of jealous rage where we find God.*

In the middle of one of my best jealous episodes, I had an encounter with God that changed everything.

Livid.
Irritated.

I felt like I constantly had to do double the amount of work to receive what others were so easily given. And I was mad.

I had it out with God one evening as I boldly yelled at Him and reminded Him of all of the times He had passed me by for others.

I felt overlooked time and time again.

I told Him about all the ways He didn't care about me or find value in me.

I accused Him of being like every other person I knew: always finding someone better than me.

It that moment He silenced me. Like a parent does to a young child, He covered my mouth with His hand and boldly interjected my words with His own:

"You don't see it, do you?"

"What?"

"Taigan, I have never bypassed you. I have been fighting for you throughout your entire life."

In that moment He took me back through four seasons of time over my life where He interjected my world and kept me close to Him. He showed me where He held me when I could have strayed.

"I have always been here waiting with my hand ready to take yours. But you need to look up and take hold of it."

He instantly gave me a mental picture. It was me walking around a huge mountain, over and over again. I was searching for something I couldn't find, and the entire time His arm was reaching down over the top of the mountain peak, waiting for me.

"You have walked around this mountain long enough. Climb up here and sit with me."

In that moment I told the Lord that I was done with whatever that mountain represented. I didn't know where to start, but I knew that I wanted His hand more than anything. Even more than my own way.

A few weeks later I had one of the most vivid dreams of my life. It was so real that I woke up sobbing, my knees so weak I could barely walk.

In the dream I was at a conference, packed with people of importance in the Christian world.

As I approached the doors to enter the auditorium, I walked past a large amount of chairs and televisions set up in the foyer area showing a live feed of the main conference stage. Those foyer seats were filled with people, so many it was surprising.

As I walked past the crowd, I peered in the small window that looked into the conference room. I saw that there were only 20 rows of chairs, all of which were filled with people who I would have considered to be better than me. Important people. More successful than me.

It infuriated me. It was obvious that this room was only for a certain calibre and the Christian commoners were only allowed to watch the conference from the feed in the foyer.

I turned around and began to walk away as it was clear that I wasn't wanted there.

In the distance I saw my husband and his friend sitting at one if the second class coffee tables. I promptly stomped over to the table.

"Can you even believe this?" I asked. "It's ridiculous. At a Christian event? Really? A VIP area that disregards a certain group of people? Oh, so only a certain handful of people get to experience the real thing, and the rest of us just get to sit out here? This is ridiculous! I'm leaving."

As I continued on, the man sitting with my husband looked at me with deep concern and, with a spark in his eye, responded to my outburst. "I think you are seeing it wrong…" he said as he got up and walked towards the auditorium door. My husband followed, and I stood there watching.

They went over to the VIP door and opened it. I looked at my husband as if to say, "You're going to get us in trouble! Get back here!"

He grinned and walked in the room, shutting the door behind him.

I walked over and just stood there for a minute. Getting the courage to put my hand on the knob, I finally opened the door. To my surprise a man greeted me.

"Ahhhh! We've been waiting for YOU!"

I stood at the back of that room for a minute, trying to see where my husband went. As I scanned the crowd, I saw him peer out into the aisle and call me down.

You have got to be kidding me! WHAT IS HE DOING?! Down in front!? No. No way.

He kept motioning me to come to the seat he saved for me. As I approached the seat, I looked around. I saw that there were many people I personally knew there smiling at me.

As I nervously went to take my seat, my husband stopped me, motioning for me to look behind him.

"Look." He grinned from ear to ear.

As I turned around I saw thousands and thousands of people in that room. Balconies upon balconies. Rows and rows. More than could ever be seen from outside in that foyer.

All ages, sizes, styles, genders, backgrounds, races. Smiling. Looking at me as if to say "Welcome. We've been waiting for you."

What I thought was a small room, only open to a select few, was actually a stadium, seating more people than I could have ever imagined.

In that moment I heard the Lord speak so clearly: *"Taigan, this room has always been open to you. But you have willingly decided to sit in the foyer and watch from a feed rather than experience it yourself. This room represents my love for you. The only difference between these people seated in this room and the ones seated in that foyer is they have opened the door. They have chosen to walk into my love instead of watching other people experience it. Everyone belongs in this room. Now go back out there and tell the rest of them."*

That dream radically changed my life. It changed the way that I saw myself and others. It has allowed me to love others more and differently than ever before. I began to understand His love for me. For all of us.

In that moment I told the Lord that I would run back out and grab as many people as I could and bring them back into that room with me.

When I woke, I had an overwhelming feeling of love. I remember crying for weeks afterwards. I felt so seen. I felt heard and cared for.

What if I told you that you aren't a second-class person?

What if I told you that you have access to the same room I do?

What if we started to believe it and live it?

What if we started to realize with our finite minds that His love is infinite, His resources are infinite, and there is more than enough to go around? He withholds no good thing.

What if that dream wasn't just for me but it was for you too?

Come with me.

Take my hand.

Follow me, I have something to show you.

There is this whole room filled with people that are full of joy and satisfied, not because of their seat in life but because of the room they sit in.

Come, there is a seat for you, too. It's right down in front, we've been saving it for you.

Come, there is One who waits for you to know and experience His love.

Come, open the door. Take YOUR seat. We've been waiting for you.

Come, experience love. It's not only for the VIP, it's for you too.

Selah

17

You Don't Know Me

It's not always in a knee bowed low, hands folded in prayer;
sometimes it is in arms crossed with our pride held high
where we find God.

By the time I reached college, I had a good chip on my shoulder—
especially when it came to church. From weird 90s youth
ministry experiences to the desire to just not think about church,
I was basically done with showing up on Sundays. I always knew and
believed that God existed; however, I thought I could put my relationship
on hold and return when it worked better for me.

The first time I met my husband (after my grandma infamously informed
me that he was a Bombay) was in the church office on a Thanksgiving
weekend when I was home from college. Thumb ring, frosted tips, and a
powder blue knit sweater. He sat on the visitor's couch thinking he was
so cool because he was a youth pastor. I couldn't stand him. He couldn't

stand me. Months later he would inform me that he thought I was a spoiled brat. I would inform him that I thought he was a pompous jerk.

Our interactions remained like that for the next year. Abrasive bickers, scathing one-liners, and the need to constantly one-up each other. (If you are part of our inner circle you are laughing right now because you know that nothing has changed! We just love each other more now.) The one thing Matt's parents always liked about me from the beginning was that I was never intimidated by his strong personality. I didn't let him get away with anything.

It wasn't until the following year that I returned home from college and infamously plopped myself down on the back pew in our church auditorium. The annual children's Christmas production was in full swing and I was over it. Yet I couldn't stay away. Even in the peak of my abrasiveness, I always returned to the church because it felt like home.

As I sat there with a glare on my face, attitude oozing from my entire being, Matthew came strutting over, pukka shell necklace and all.

He annoyingly sat down beside me then turned and stared at me for an uncomfortable amount of time. (He still does this when he has something he needs to say.) I rolled my head in his direction and with a friendly, "What? Can I help you with something?" My life was about to change.

"You realize you are going to hell, right?"

"Excuse me?"

"Well, you aren't walking with Jesus, and the last time I checked my Bible... wait let me check it again... *pause*... yep, hell."

I was livid. I never had someone taken such a hard stance and call me out like that in my entire life. I still remember saying "Who do you think you are? You don't even know me. You're such a jerk."

He proceeded to follow me around the church for the rest of the night, smirking, while I glared at him, hoping he would take a hint and hit the road.

> Disclaimer: This is not the best way to deal with someone, when it comes to their relationship with the Lord. To this day, my husband has never spoke to another person like this, especially when it comes to their faith walk. He remembers sitting beside me, and the Lord telling Him to be as blunt as possible with me, to call me out on my stuff. Little did he know that his approach was actually the best way to interact with me. As much as I pretended to hate it, I still remember feeling seen by God. It was in that moment I felt important that someone would tell me that there was more for me.

It took me a week after that interaction to fall asleep peacefully, without having the TV on to distract me from my thoughts. I was overcome with conviction. My life was disrupted and I knew it needed to change. I just didn't know how. I also knew that I didn't want to go back to Sunday school rules and religious expectations. There had to be something more.

As much as I hate telling this story because I know it makes my husband sound abrasive, I am so thankful for this moment in my journey. I am not sure where I would be in my life if he didn't have the guts to sit down beside me that night and say the unpopular thing.

I had no idea that our relationship with evolve past irritation. I had no idea that a return to Christ would be the beginning of ministry. I had no idea that as exciting as the future would be, it would also be equally as challenging.

Often times we tiptoe around people and their feelings. We are afraid of offending them and making them uncomfortable. We want to be polite and not step on any toes. The last time I checked, the kingdom of God was an upside down and backwards kingdom. Jesus rarely spoke to make people comfortable. He said things that offended people, and yet it always called them higher.

I could have chosen to write Matt off that day. I could have reduced that moment to a really irritating interaction with a big-mouthed youth pastor; however, I learned that the Lord doesn't always speak in whispers and nudges. Sometimes He gets His point across in offensive truths and harsh one-liners.

By the spring I had removed a lot of the hindrances to my walk with the Lord from my life. I've learned more about doing the right thing and doing it well since then. I found myself understanding what it meant to have a personal relationship with God, not just a religious weekly interaction.

The irony was that although Matt didn't know me, the Lord did. He knew exactly what I needed. He knew the way that I needed to hear the important things. He knew the timing and he knew the timeline. He knew that although I wasn't known by this stranger with a big opinion, one day they would become the person that knows me best.

Sometimes the way the Lord intervenes isn't conventional. It is not always how we assume Him to be. Often times he shows up in unexpected places, through unexpected people.

I am thankful that the Lord spoke to my future husband that day. I am thankful that Matt had the discernment to speak what He felt the Lord was saying, even though it seemed crazy and unconventional.

I am thankful that even though I was unknown, I was seen.

Selah

18

Wedding Bells

It's not always in mid-life milestones and
perfectly curated timelines; sometimes it is as a naive bride
where we find God.

When we decided to get married, people thought we were crazy. I was only 21 and had quickly gone from not being able to stand Matt to not being able to stay away from him. As much as I knew it was crazy and that people would be nervous for us, I knew it was right.

I knew it was right because up until that point in my life, the thought of marrying someone one day terrified me. I would talk about it because it seemed like the right thing to dream about, but truthfully, I always saw myself living alone (or with my best friend Nancy) for the rest of my life.

I guess that's the thing about our hard stances and abrasive takes on life.

Often times—at least for me—God has shown up in the midst of them, and taught me there was something more than what I envisioned for myself.

For me, Matt was like coming home. I loved that he was a man of God, even if I had to take the pastoral stuff with it. I loved that he was assertive and could take charge of any situation. I loved that he was extra social and could bring energy to the room. I am not denying that there was some dependance there; however, when I met him I knew that my life would never be dull. And I liked that.

About ten years after we were married, someone told me that they didn't think we would make it past a year. Another person told me that I would be pregnant within six months of marriage and that my aspirations for more than motherhood would be done. Both people barely knew me. I quickly came to realize that people decide whatever they want to think about you and that's okay. Whether they thought we were too young or thought they knew what our life would end up looking like it wasn't up to me to prove them wrong. I was only responsible for tending to my life and producing what I envisioned for us.

For all of the stigma and stereotypes that came with being a young couple that got married quickly, there has been so much reward. I am certainly not the same person I was in 2006, and neither is he, but the journey has taken two very stubborn, strong willed, opinionated kids, and created an adventurous life.

Our marriage is far from perfect. He's an outwardly dominant and strong personality. I am too, I'm just passive about it. Our personalities tend to switch in their dominance when we get stressed. I get loud, and he gets quiet. We are not traditional in anything we do and I am sure people wonder how we have lived together this long or if we even like each other. I can assure you, we do.

If there is anything that I have come to learn over the last fifteen years it is this: there is no map for marriage. No journey looks the same, feels the same, or has the same destination. What works for me, would likely never work for you, and that's okay.

Alternatively, I have come to peace with the realization that my marriage isn't anyone else's. I once thought that if my husband didn't do all of the things or say all of the things that so and so's husband did, it must mean our relationship wasn't healthy.

So often we disregard the positives in our own lives, because we think they are less valuable than the characteristics others possess. My husband doesn't dote on me 24/7, but he wakes up happy almost every day and is the most consistent person I know. For me that is a dream come true. Marriage has brought me more than a partner and someone to grow old with; it has taught me about sacrifice, graciousness, and steadfastness.

What most people thought was a young life forfeited for marriage, has been a young life saved by sacrificial love. I have learned more about my faith through my marriage than anything else I've experienced.

In all of my naivety I never knew how much growing I had to do. Year after year, the Lord has shown up and taught us about His love through our very own.

As a young 21 year old girl, I believed that I had just found someone to share life with, and yet all of these years later I can see with hindsight that I was given another way to find God.

Selah

19

Many Things

*It's not always in the middle of a Sunday
morning church service; sometimes it is
in the midnight hour where we find God.*

A number of years ago, I woke up in the middle of the night and found myself under complete spiritual attack. I was up for almost two hours fighting the anxiety and anger that suddenly came over me.

"You're annoying. Ugly. Fat. An awful wife and ministry partner. Moody. Dumb. Nobody cares about what you say or think. Too far gone. Too much. Not enough. Attention seeking. Fake. Opinionated…"

After about an hour of listening to this narrative, I finally remembered to ask the Lord what *He* was saying:

"You are concerned with many things. But what is most important? You'll have to decide if you are going to believe what those lies are saying, or if you'll believe me."

His words pierced through my very core.

Do you know the verse?

> *"Martha, Martha, you are worried and bothered and anxious about so many things; but only one thing is necessary, for Mary has chosen the good part that which is to her advantage, which will not be taken away from her."* Luke 10:41-42

While Martha was anxious about many things, Mary chose the one thing that was to her advantage: listening intently at the feet of Jesus, hanging on to every word He said.

That is something that the enemy can never take from us.

I had to pray through this verse for almost an hour and this is where I landed: whenever my will, desire, emotions, pride, and selfishness get put in the place where only He should be, I give the enemy an entrance point.

My mind, thoughts, and emotions had become so focused on me that I no longer had things in the right order. I found myself no longer sitting at His feet, but rather sitting at the feet of my own pride.

Instead of listening and hanging on His every word, I had become worried by many things. These are indications that He is no longer where He should be in my life.

The enemy would love for us to get into a place of fear, loathing, and anger.

The enemy would love for us to get depressed and anxious about many things.

The enemy would love to keep us up in the middle of the night so that we spend the next day tired, grumpy, and sad.

The enemy would love for us to get our eyes off Jesus and focused on ourselves.

He knows that is what renders us powerless.

When you are worried and bothered by many things, remember the most important thing.

Decide if you are going to dwell on what others think about you.

Decide if you are going to choose to believe what He says about you.

Take a step back and see where you are sitting. If it's at the seat of your pride or problem, you're going to have to get up and get back to the right place: seated at the feet of Jesus.

That is where peace will return, hearts will align, grace will flow, and perfect love will cast out fear.

Selah

20

Don't Rush

It's not always in the hustle and bustle of everyday life;
sometimes it is in the slowing down where we find God.

When I had my son, my sister-in-law called and told me that from now on my life motto would have to be: I am not in a rush.

Resolving to not be in a rush was one of the biggest adjustments I would have to make as I entered motherhood. Nothing was easy anymore. I had to plan. I couldn't just do what I wanted when I wanted. On top of that, as someone that needed 'alone time' to survive, it became clear that I was never going to be alone again.

I have always been in a rush. It was one of the biggest criticisms I would receive every year when I got my report card: "Taigan's work would be much cleaner and thorough if she slowed down and didn't rush to complete it."

I have felt this in my professional life, in ministry, motherhood, marriage, and life in general. I can feel myself getting anxious, rushing a process or wishing time away, always wanting and waiting to 'get on with it.' Sometimes just shutting down, resolving to come back to reality when reality finally looked how I wanted it to.

Over the last number of years I have felt the Lord teaching me about process.

Waiting. Patience. Slowing down. Trusting His timing. Living in the moment.

I had to ask the Lord forgive me for being idealistic.
For believing that life could start when I got all of my stuff sorted out.
For the inability to find joy until this or that worked itself out.
For refusing to live in peace because the process didn't look how I thought
    it should.

I am the girl that refused to hang a mirror or picture in my previous home for close to two years because it wasn't going to be my 'forever home.'

I have learned that when we try and take things out of their season and rush them we end up spoiling the fruit.

I have learned that although His intentions are for good and that He is faithful to complete all that he has promised, He has a process.

I have learned that He's more concerned about who I am becoming than what I get out of the deal.

I have learned that He's more concerned about revealing Himself through me than proving Himself to me.

I have learned that He's not in a rush.

I have felt the hand of the Lord push me to be at peace with the coming and going of everyday life. I have felt Him nudge me into releasing the need for the excitement of the new to keep me content.

I have heard Him speak so clearly: *"I'm not in a rush, and neither are you."*

My need to rush through is in the desire to selfishly get on to the things that make me happy, forgetting that sooner or later they always come around so I may as well have peace in the process. No matter how long the process is.

> *"These things I plan won't happen right away. Slowly, steadily, surely, the time approaches when the vision will be fulfilled. If it seems slow, do not despair, for these things will surely come to pass. Just be patient! They will not be overdue a single day!"*
> Habakkuk 2:3

Whatever you are waiting on or whatever season you are in, God will not be overdue a single day. He's not in a rush, and His timing is always perfect.

His process brings good, thoroughly thought-out plans.

Take what you can from the season you are in and tend to it.
Dream about what you want for the future and pray for it.
Listen for His voice in the moment and act on it.

Slowly, steadily, surely.

God says, "I am not in a rush"—so slow down.

He won't bypass you.

He is not in a rush and neither are you.

Selah

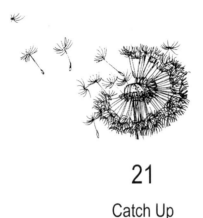

21

Catch Up

*It's not always in milestones of success and keeping
up with the Jones'; sometimes it is in our
feelings of inadequacy where we find God.*

The first time I felt like I was getting behind in life was in my twenty-seventh year of life. After a woman told me that they thought I was going to be pregnant within six months of marriage, I did everything in my power to prove them (and anyone else that had the same thought) wrong. I spent many years happy and proud of my ability to not get pregnant, enjoying our early years of marriage and becoming established.

Then it happened.

Somewhere between marriage and motherhood, Facebook landed, which meant the inner workings of other people's lives became more mainstream. Suddenly it was as if every person I knew was having more and more children, and if I didn't have Facebook, I would have never known.

I remember the day that I saw someone in my age range post that they are having another baby. Their fourth. My heart started racing. I broke out into a cold sweat and my stomach started to turn. *What am I doing with my life? These people had four kids in the last 5 years, and all I have done is get married and finished school.* The comparison crept in and fear began to take over.

Am I behind? Is my life, at the spinster age of 26, over? What am I waiting for? Am I selfish for not having any kids yet?

Questions circled my mind and I began to panic to the point of anger. I grabbed my phone, ran downstairs, and told Matt to turn off the TV.

"That's it. We're having a baby!"

A look of shock and confusion washed over his face, as I turned my phone towards him to reveal the pregnancy announcement. "Have you seen this?"

"Seen what?

"This."

"Oh, no, I haven't. Yay! They're having a baby!"

"Yeah, their fourth…"

"Is that a problem for you?"

"Well, yes. But only because I haven't had any yet. I am so close to her age. She's done so much more than me. Maybe I should just get it over with and have a baby. I'm getting old."

"Well, you just let me know when you are sure about that and we can talk."

He didn't seem to be flustered, and yet he was five years older than me. In an instant everything I had been proud of and content with changed. Years later we know that social media is a powerful, dangerous, double-edged sword. What can bring people with the largest distances together, can also separate the closest of friends—all because of misunderstandings, misread tones, and comparison.

My friend's intention wasn't to make me feel inadequate, jealous, or angry. Those feelings were sparked because of my unknown insecurity about keeping up with others. Over the years, especially when it comes to social media, I have learned to recognize when I am feeling dissatisfied with my personal life, social circle, spiritual condition, or physical health, because often times what surfaces are feelings of jealousy, irritation, and inadequacy.

When we are secure in who we are and what we have, those feelings towards others and what they post, rarely exist. If I am happy and content with what I have right now, still dreaming for the future without getting mad when others reach those goals before me, it's a sign of spiritual maturity and trust.

Panic, anxiety, and fear over what others have or accomplish is distrust in the plan that He has for you. It's fear that our lives aren't as valuable. It's worry that we are being left behind as the world around us progresses. Can I tell you something? You will not be forgotten and you will not be left in the dust of your peers.

None of us start at the same takeoff line. No two journeys are the same. What makes us believe that our destination points are any different? We are not meant to keep up with one another. We are meant to rejoice with one another in our peaks and mourn with one another in our valleys.

A sign of spiritual maturity is when you start to pray, believe in and hope the best for the people around you, even if it means feeling like you are being left behind in the dust of their success. I use to pray that my peers wouldn't get ahead of me and that I would reach milestones of success before they did. Now I pray that all of their dreams and goals come true. I actively call out the names of the people in my closest circle in prayer and ask that God would bless them. Now I get excited when I hear that they got a new shiny toy or their kid won a medal.

Friendship is about believing the best about others and hoping the best for them too. What stopped me in my tracks almost ten years ago and made me boil with rage was only the beginning of a long journey towards becoming a person that could move beyond feelings of inadequacy and inferiority.

I have learned over the years that there is no such thing as catching up—there is only His timing. It's never late. It's never too soon. It's never off track. What feels like setbacks are often preparations.

If you feel off track, it's time to align yourself with the One that is guiding you. Your life isn't about catching up or keeping up. It's about staying in step with Him.

Perfect cadence. Perfect timing.

Selah

22

Wait Here

*It's not always in our moments of serene meditation
and peaceful prayer; sometimes it is in a hysterical child
on your front lawn where we find God.*

A number of years ago as I was watching YouTube videos in bed, I heard an interaction between a young boy and an adult woman outside my window.

He approached her as she was walking her dogs and asked for help. His mom was out for a bike ride and he was afraid that she had forgotten about him at his friend's house.

"I don't have a phone with me," she said. "Can you wait here until I run to my house to get my cell? I'll come back here, and we can call her."

"Okay."

"Do you know your mom's phone number?"

"Yes. I am just scared because she left me at her friend's house and now I think she forgot about me."

Back and forth, the conversation went in circles while her dogs growled and barked. After a few minutes of listening to their conversation, I got out of my bed and ran downstairs.

I burst out the front door, determined to fix the situation. "Hi. I'm sorry but I was listening to you from my bedroom. I have a phone. What's your mom's number?"

He was at least 13 years old, which meant to me that he was definitely old enough to be left alone.

"Ugh. I just don't think she will answer. She's riding her bike."

"Well, do you have her number?" I asked, irritation settling into my tone.

"Yeah." He pulled a piece of paper from his pocket with a number scribbled in pencil on it. My mind raced with all the possible scenarios I could be facing.

I was certain this kid was pulling one over on me. Convinced he was going to ask to use the phone and then run away with it. The worst possible situations bombarded my thoughts.

"Let me see it. I will call her. What's her name?"

"She isn't going to answer. I am just worried that she is going to forget about me."

"Give. Me. The. Paper." Pointed, direct, and said through gritted teeth. My mom tone was in full effect.

I dialled his mother's number and after a couple of rings she answered:

"Hello!?"

I could hear an echo, the kind you get when the person you are talking to is in the same room.

"Son! What are you doing!?"

I turned and saw her approaching us on her bike, phone held to her ear.

"I told you to stay inside and that I would be back! You are a big boy now. What are you doing?"

As she got closer, I could see her concern. It was obvious she had been clear with him about where she was going and what she was doing. From a mother to a mother, I could tell that she had clearly told him what he should do as he was waiting.

He was just relieved that she returned.

As she consoled him, I began to walk away and she yelled down the sidewalk: "Thank you! Thank you miss, I am so sorry about all of this!"

"No problem…" I said with a chuckle.

As I closed the door behind me, I heard the Holy Spirit whisper to my heart:

"That is what I am saying to you."

How often do we hear something from the Lord, read about his promises, or witness His faithfulness, only to walk away and forget?

He gives us His number.
Tells us that He will be right back.

Asks us to wait a bit.
Reminds us that we are more than able to.
And then we forget.

We get panicked and start running around trying to figure out what to do when He's already told us what to do: wait patiently.

That's fine for a bit, but then when it takes longer than we thought, gets dark, or we get worked up in fear, we forget about His nature and we find ourselves outside on the street, waving dog ladies down.

We find ourselves asking for help that we really don't need because all we really want is to be comforted and safe.

I saw myself so clearly in that moment. I am sure the Lord often looks at me and says: *"What are you doing? Didn't I tell you...?"* as he wraps His arm around me and walks me back into the house.

He is faithful to do what He has said He will do.

He knows that we are capable of patience.

He has given us everything we need and He tucks it in our pocket.

Be reminded of His faithfulness when you find yourself out on the street, waving down a dog lady in a panic because you feel forgotten and lost.

He is right down the street, coming in hot on His pedal bike.

Phone to His ear, answering our call.

Selah

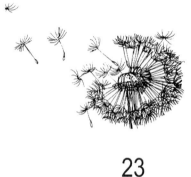

23

Battle Cry

*It's not always new ideas or first heard words; sometimes
it is in repetition and persistence where we find God.*

Have you ever heard something a million times and it never
registered until suddenly… it did?

A few years ago, I heard a church message on worship and it suddenly all
made sense.

The speaker talked about how worship releases something in the
atmosphere.

Strongholds break.
Breakthrough happens.
Things change.

In that moment I heard the Lord whisper: *"worship is a battle cry."*

Worshipping in the midst of the storm.
Praising before the breakthrough.
High praise in low moments.
It is all warfare.

In that moment my brain did a rewind and I was taken back to October of 2015 when I attended a women's worship night at a local church.

Something broke in my life that evening and seeds were planted for the fruit I am harvesting today.

I always believed in God. I had experienced His goodness. I believed that He existed but I never had a personal 'a ha' moment.

I use to pray that I would know that I know that I know… that He was real. I prayed that He would be so real to me that I would be moved by my revelation. I prayed that when I sang the songs of worship they would be more than words. I prayed that they would be testimony.

"I don't know how you will get me there, but I want to know you personally and authentically."

I have always counted that cold October night as a changing point in my life. I had never experienced worship like I did that night. It was as if everything slowed right down and the room became very still. Quiet. Personal. In that moment there was clarity and I came face to face with a God that I was accustomed to just singing about.

It's impossible to encounter Him and not be changed.

As I walked away from that evening, I didn't know that it would begin a series of breakthroughs in my life.

I didn't notice it right away, but in hindsight, I see it all so clearly.

Worship is a battle cry.

It declares war on the enemy.
It proclaims breakthrough that has not yet come.
It gathers all of the broken and defeated and says: here is your victory.

Not because of our act of worship, but because of our acknowledgment of His goodness.

It takes our eyes off of us and it magnifies the One who stands in the gap for all of our issues, problems, and shortcomings.

That night set the stage for a season of breakthrough in my life. It declared war on the plans created by the enemy.

It set me free.

It ignited a passion.

It released the things that had held me tightly for so long.

When you are in the biggest fight of your life: worship.
When you don't know what to do next: worship.
When you don't have the answers: worship.
When you haven't seen your breakthrough: worship.
When you feel like your hands are tied: lift those bad boys over your head and worship.

Worship is a battle cry.

High praise in low moments is warfare.

It tears down walls.
It breaks chains.
It sets us free.

Selah

24

Leave Your Life

It's not always in our clenched fists
and tightly held grip; often times it is in our open hands
and acts of surrender where we find God.

I had a dream that I was at a conference and a man pointed me out of the crowd and told me had a word for me.

As he approached with tears in his eyes, he placed his hands on my shoulders and simply said: *"Leave your life."*

Leave your life? What?

I waited for a minute as he stood there holding my shoulders in silence. Surely there was more than that.

Leave your life.

Walk away? End it? Run away?

It didn't seem godly or even practical. In my dream I started to reason through it with the people around me:

"I think he said 'leave your life…' "

"I know, I did too, but I think he MEANT live your life."

"I heard LEAD your life."

Sometimes when God speaks it moves beyond human reasoning; in fact, that's when it is most profound. As someone who always wants to know the who, what, when, where, why, and how—God often speaks to me in ways that I'm not looking for.

Leave your life.

As I started to reason with the Lord and ask Him what it meant, I heard Him whisper: *"pick up your cross."*

"Okay, so what am I doing here? Laying something down or picking something up? I can't do two things at once. I'm really not the best multitasker."

"Exactly. Leave your life. Lay it down so you can pick up your cross."

Do you know it?

> *"If you want to follow Me, you must deny yourself the things you think you want. You must pick up your cross and follow Me. The person who wants to save his life must lose it, and she who loses her life for Me will find it. Look, does it make sense to truly become successful, but then to hand over your very soul? What is your soul really worth?"* Matthew 16:24-26

I've been really stuck on myself lately.

What I want.
What I need to be happy.
What I want my life to look like.
What I think should happen.
Where I think I can thrive.
What I need to be doing to feel successful.

I was at the end of my rope in self loathing and sadness because I felt like I was so hard done by.

The Lord completely intercepted my thought life and said: *"Stop. Leave it. Lay it down. Let me show you what happiness and success and living really is…"*

Get your eyes off of yourself.

Stop trying to plan and scheme and rationalize your way through everything.

Leave your life.

Not behind.

Don't wash your hands of it.

Lay it down at the feet of Jesus and leave it there so you can pick up your cross, and let Him lead you into a life that is far greater than the one you are holding on so tightly to.

Selah

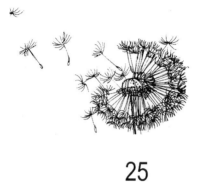

25

Hindsight

*It's not always in perfectly prepared sermons
or eloquently written books; sometimes it is in the back
of a chaotic raft where we find God.*

Back in the fall of 2009, my husband and I signed up to take some youth white-water rafting down the Ottawa River.

I didn't really know what I had signed up for when it came to the whole retreat. I honestly thought it was going to be a few Walmart blowup rafts and a leisurely float down the river. I was shocked and terrified when I showed up that cold fall day and realized what was ahead of me.

I will never forget all of the rules and instructions they had as we showed up to the site to get our wetsuits and helmets; as we lined up trying to get in our boats; as we began to paddle and I realized how hard it was.

It was terrifying. I had never been so scared and tired in all of my life. Within minutes of paddling, I realized how out of shape I was. I realized how afraid I was of water and being out of control. I realized how powerful the current was and that I wasn't as powerful as I thought I was. I realized I wasn't really cut out for life beyond sitting in a lawn chair when it came to the great outdoors.

When I look back now, I am glad that I had the experience. I am glad that I have the memories. And I am glad that I went in blindly, not know what I was getting into—because if I had, I wouldn't have signed up at all.

As I remembered that rafting experience I felt the Lord remind me how I had that exact same experience when I married someone in pastoral ministry.

Back in 2005, I remember hearing the Lord ask me if I was ready for the life before me as I read my Bible in my grandparent's apartment.

"Are you sure you are ready for this?"

"Yep. I'm sure. It will be fine! Let's just get this show on the road."
—Me, age 21

I remember pleading my case with Joyce Meyer playing on a VHS in the background. Telling Him what I was made of (like He didn't already know).

I had suddenly gone from a girl adamant that she would never marry a pastor to being the girl who was made for it.

I look back at that time and I realize I was just like future 2009-Ottawa-River-me: the one that would show up with hardly any supplies or knowledge for a day of white-water rafting, down an intense river; the one that showed up with hardly a care in the world, who was just there for whatever came her way; the one that showed up and as she was being pushed off the shore and down the river she began to realize what was about to happen.

It was bigger than her.
It was going to be hard.
It was more than she had signed up for.
It was out of her control.
It involved a wet suit and a helmet. (Lord, help me.)

There are so many things in life that we can't understand until we experience them ourselves. We say "yes" blindly, thinking that we have all the answers and tenacity to remain steadfast under whatever comes our way. The reality is that we don't even know what's waiting on the other side of our yes, let alone what we are capable of handling.

If I had known what was waiting for me on the other side of my pleading some 16 years ago, I likely would have run.

Not because of people, or church, or ministry, but because of what I would have seen in myself.

What I would need to work through.

What attitudes I would be struggling with.

What work He would need to do in me to prepare me for life and ministry.

I smile when I think about myself back then.

Without the experience itself, I likely would have run at the idea of it.

Now, having experienced firsthand what I couldn't see coming and what I hadn't prepared for, I wouldn't change a thing.

It's the grace of God. To be able to walk through some stuff and then turn around and say thank you because I see what You were doing.

You're making me wiser.
You're giving me experience.
You're teaching me about love.
You're walking with me.
You're more concerned about who I am becoming than how I get there.

You're in it all and I am better because of it.

If I knew that September day what I had signed up for, I wouldn't have gotten off the bus. But as I approached the raft and jumped in, I experienced something that can never be taken from me.

I think the Lord is asking us to say "yes" without the knowledge of what's on the other side.

Simply put, it's faith.

Put on your wetsuit.

Fasten your helmet.

Get in the raft.

Let Him push you off the shore.

Selah

26

Bold Yes

It's not always in our confident response or quick results; sometimes it is in our second guessing and shaky steps of faith where we find God.

A number of years ago I felt the Lord ask me to do something as an act of obedience. I said yes. Ever since, I can honestly say that I have felt like it was a curse in disguise.

It's heartbreaking, discouraging, and exhausting to live in those kinds of decisions: you think they are going to turn out one way and they go in the complete opposite direction.

Had I heard wrong?

Was I just deep in a season of depression and anxiety and not thinking straight?

Was it all my own idea?

I have been reviewing this "thing" over and over in my head and I would be lying if I said I haven't fought off feelings of anger towards God.

"I did what I thought You told me to do. I was taking a step of faith. Why did You ask me to do this? I feel like You did it just to push me or to show my true colours. That You wanted to rub all of my past mistakes in my face. I get it now. You wanted to prove a point. Thanks."

That has been my ongoing internal conversation with the Lord.

A moment came when I felt it come full circle. With instant, hot tears running down my face, I heard in my spirit:

"I didn't ask you to make that decision to ruin you, curse you, or make your life miserable. I asked you to make that decision so that your bold "yes" would be an act of obedience and a testimony of your faith in Me. It was an opportunity to live out your willingness to follow where I lead."

For a very brief moment it all made sense in my spirit. What the human mind cannot understand can be revealed through the Holy Spirit so that we can see with divine wisdom. In that moment it made sense. I got it. And for the first time in a very long time I felt thankful for the decision instead of regretful.

Who knows what that "yes" has brought to my life. It could have been a stepping stone to other miracles and insights that I have had the blessing of saying "yes" to. Who knows what it will bring in the future. I do know that when we see those moments as something to be treasured, more will come.

"No one who is tempted should ever be confused and say that God is testing him. The One who created us is free from evil and can't be tempted, so He doesn't tempt anyone." James 1:13

Lord, forgive me for believing that You didn't have my best interest at hand.

Forgive me for believing that it was all a set up.

Forgive me for the way I have responded in moments of frustration, anger, and pain.

Help me to see Your purposes for the things You ask me to do.

Help me to remember that it is never You that is tempting me, but rather You're revealing what's already deeply rooted within me so that I can be pruned to flourish in ways that only You can do.

Help me live out the rest of this season in patience and righteousness until You say it is over.

You are good and Your purposes for me are good.

Thank you for being gracious enough to remind me when I have believed the lie that You are anything but those things.

Selah

27

By Your Fruit

*It's not always in the things that we post or share on
social media; it is always in the fruit of our lives where we find God.*

My husband and I often talk about ministry and the perception that people give with their online presence. He has always struggled with this because he just isn't the type to go on social media and share every little thing he is doing with the world. He is wired very differently than me, so when we have these discussions it usually leaves me mulling over his words for some time. Here's what he said:

"Just because people post more doesn't mean they are doing more. Just because you can't see it doesn't mean it's not happening. Just because it looks perfect, it doesn't mean that it is. Just because it appears that others don't go through stuff, it doesn't mean that they don't. Just because I'm not wired like so and so, it doesn't mean that I am less than.

Because of today's society and social media we have this idea that if we don't see something happening, obviously they aren't doing anything of value. That's just not true. For many years people did a lot of things for God and they didn't have a social media following to share it with. Yet, it still happened, and somehow, someway (insert sarcasm here), God used them."

As he left the house I felt the Lord echo his words: *"He's right."*

Me: *I feel like You are going to elaborate...*

God: *I didn't say 'they will know you by your online presence, I said 'they will know you by your fruit.'*

Me: *I hate when You're right.*

What does that look like?

> *"But the fruit produced by the Holy Spirit within you is divine love in all its varied expressions: joy that overflows, peace that subdues, patience that endures, kindness in action, a life full of virtue, faith that prevails, gentleness of heart strength of spirit. They are meant to be limitless." Galatians 5:22-23*

Let's stop being people that look for fruit in the superficial.

You won't find it there.

Selah

28

Enjoy Ministry

*It's not always in our moments of quiet solitude
and reflection; sometimes it is in our one on one
encounters with people of influence where we find God.*

"**W**hat is the Lord saying to you right now? What's the thing that He keeps pressing over and over in your life?"

I stared across the room at this beautiful, seasoned pastor's wife as she picked my brain and my heart.

I thought that we were here to learn.

I thought that this was going to be about logistics.

I thought that this was just a means to an end.

Now here I was. Alone in a room. One on one. And she wasn't asking superficial fluff anymore. She wasn't just assessing my actions or subtle remarks. She was getting to the heart.

"He's saying..."

I paused and looked at the picture on the wall. Afraid to make eye contact because I didn't actually know what was going to come out of my mouth next.

"He's saying it's okay to enjoy ministry."

I turned my head and stared her dead in the eyes, shocked by my own words but playing it cool.

Her mouth dropped.

Her eyes dramatically closed.

She let out a noise that almost sounded painful.

My heart began to race.

Oh no. That was a bad answer. What was the right answer? Why did I say that? Where did that come from!? Ugh. What's she writing down now…?

"WOW!"

"Wow?"

"WOW! I've been in ministry for over twenty-five years and I think that is one of the most profound things I have ever heard!"

"It is?"

"Yes. It is. You need to tell people that. You need to tell other women in ministry that, okay?"

"Okay?"

I realized that my answer wasn't a one-off.

It wasn't by chance. It wasn't a fluke.

It was something that the Lord has been pressing over and over in my life. Like a toddler that wants a snack. Relentlessly.

As my mind spun through the Rolodex of words He had been speaking to me, I began to see that He's had one goal in mind: to soften my sharp edges and shape me into who He created me to be.

Someone He can use.

We are all on a journey. But I knew that this was some "above and beyond" sort of stuff for me.

The truth is that for years I wouldn't allow myself to enjoy ministry because I had been fed a lie that it wasn't suppose to be enjoyable.

Less than.
Negative.
A target.
Annoying.
People are hard to deal with.
I'm not cut out for it.

These were the list of cons that I would cycle through on a daily basis and over time I became resentful. I felt entitled to something different. I became skeptical. I wanted to be anything other than a pastor's wife.

But that was the problem. That box. It wasn't made for me. It never has been and it never will be. And that's okay.

That is what He started to reveal.

Can we just have some real talk?

Do you know why I struggled with that title so much? Because I knew I was a leader in my own right. I knew that I had a ministry beyond being a supportive spouse. I knew I wasn't fulfilling my own call and so I resented anything that showed up and tried to label me.

For most of my married life I believed that I wasn't allowed to enjoy ministry or claim my specific calling because I didn't go to Bible college. It has hindered me and weighed on me for years. And so instead of just accepting that God called me to be an awesome partner to my husband, I decided to wear it like a badge, claiming that I wanted nothing to do with any of it anyways. My favourite line use to be "I didn't go to Bible college for a reason..."

That was a lie and it came from the depths of my insecurity and fear.

And so here I am. As I watch my journey unfold. As I grow up. As I learn more about who I am. As I ask Him to come and speak to the hidden places of my heart.

Here I am. Realizing that nothing is by chance. And nothing is wasted. That everything along the road to today has been milestones and markers that are only making me into who He destined me to be.

Multi-faceted. Complex. Ever-changing. A voice. Called to live authentically. That in itself is a personal ministry.

I walked away from the experience with that woman and I felt my armour fall off. The wall that I had built around me crumbled. I laid my weapons down at His feet.

"Here. I don't need these anymore." I pushed them across the floor like chips in a poker match.

In that moment I felt the presence of the Lord wrap around me like one of those giant inflatable balls you squeeze into and get rolled around in. I saw a picture of darts and arrows flying towards me, bouncing off one by one as they hit His presence.

I walked away from that experience a little taller and a little stronger. I felt a little softer and a little lighter. I walked away more confident than ever before.

I felt my need to defend myself fall away, as I fell into the arms of my Defender.

Freedom came in acknowledging the repetitive whisper of my heart: it's okay to enjoy the journey. You don't have to earn it. Or deserve it. You don't have to apologize for it. Or prove yourself. It's yours. Please take it and enjoy it.

Selah

29

Those Were the Days

It's not always in our well deserved moments of alone time and selfish desires fulfilled; sometimes it is in the unending tasks and countless needs from children where we find God.

It's 10:05 p.m. I am finally alone and not tending to a small child.

I'll make this quick, because 6 a.m. shows up real fast and before I know it the big kid is going to be passive aggressively nudging his knee into my back until I wake up. He needs cereal. And a show. Oh, and he doesn't want to be alone on the main floor so even though the baby is still sleeping, it's still time to get up.

As I was frustrated with a baby that fought sleep (even though I was clearly ready for bed an hour before) I whispered something under my breath:

"Oh yes. I'll remember these days. These are the days that pushed me to my breaking point."

I remember those days as a new mom. I wasn't as prepared for parenting like I am now. Sure, I still have moments where I dramatically proclaim "I'm done!" but the difference is now I have a history to tell me that it won't always be like this.

For me, the biggest surprise of motherhood was the reality that I was never off the hook and able to do my own thing ... ever again. It doesn't matter how many times you tell a new parent that, they won't truly understand it until the baby is there and in front of them. Until it cries and they can't hand it off to someone else. Until they are so tired that all they want to do is crawl under the covers and sleep, but they can't. You can't You are it.

I remember crying in my bed, under the covers, exhausted and unprepared for the never-ending role of motherhood. "I can't do this. I wasn't ready for this. I need someone to rescue me." These were the things that ran through my mind over and over.

I think a lot of moms find themselves in some sort of postpartum state like this. Maybe we don't have language for it. Maybe we've never wanted to admit it. Maybe we've felt bad or guilty for having those feelings. Maybe we thought we were the only ones.

The more women I talk to, the more I realize that we aren't alone. Whether it's a newborn or a school-aged child, we all struggle with the same worries, doubts, guilt, exhaustion, and fears. None of us are immune to it.

I am not in a depressed or anxious state. This isn't a cry for help. This isn't a red flag.

This is a testimony for the mom who thinks they are alone. This is for the mom that is scared to do it again. This is for the mom that feels guilty because she isn't one hundred percent on all the time.

You are normal and you are not alone.

I can speak from a history with God. Those days are few. They feel long but they will one day be a faint memory. He will bring you through and you will walk out on the other side, ready and equipped to face another one. To do it all over. Again and again. Day after day.

And when you think it will never end.
That you'll never sleep again.
That you will never have a moment to breathe peacefully.
That you will never be in a room alone again. (Where are my introverts at!?)

He will remind you of these days.

These days when He taught you about unconditional, relentless, selfless, unwavering love.

These days when He taught you about commitment. Covenant. Family.

These days when He taught you to strengthen yourself in Him.

These days when He taught you that you had everything it takes to wake up day after day and do it all over again.

Rest well. Tomorrow is a new day.

Selah

30

It's a Process

*It's not always in our euphoria and dreams fulfilled; sometimes
it is in the process of walking out our pain where we find God.*

I wonder how much of our pain is actually just process in disguise.

The Lord has been working on me. I still have a lot of ideas about
how I think things should look, pan out, and fall in line for me. I've had a
lot of moments where God has nabbed me by the back the neck and
brought me up high, away from my perspective, so He could show me
the bigger picture from the sky.

I'm realizing that most of the things I have selfishly categorized as
inconvenience or pain have actually just been personal irritations and
matters of personal preference.

I should be able to...

I wanted this to happen...
I don't deserve this...
I am mad about...
I have endured this long enough...

I like to call it pain, but really it's just process.

The pressing.
The crushing.
The irritating.

They're all just processes that are used to form us into who we are meant
to be.

Showing us how much we can endure.
Shaping us into something a little more appealing.
Softening our edges so we become a little less abrasive.
Scaling us back so we can see with perspective where it all actually lands
    in the bigger picture.

If I truly knew the pain and suffering of another person, I would probably
be quick to embrace my own journey. I would probably even be thankful
for it too.

It's never as bad as it seems.

It's never as far gone as it looks.

It's never as urgent as it feels.

It's never so much about the short term pain, but it's more about the
process of getting to where we were meant to be.

Selah

31

Take Root

It's not in the constant uprooting and re-homing; it is in the digging down deep and taking root where we find God.

In March of 2017 I bought myself a little monogramed plate from Anthropology. I was at a conference in Vancouver, and as I always do, I made it my mission to find the mall as soon as I had some down time.

Over the past few years it has become my custom to pick up something like this, as well as a perfume, when I am in a city that has an Anthropology. It's one of my favourite stores, and since Saskatoon doesn't have one, it always feels right to treat myself.

Every night I take off my wedding rings and earrings and I place them on this plate. It serves as a reminder of the day I bought it. The day I found myself walking around aimlessly trying to find something new with a

"T" on it that wasn't another coffee mug.

"Ooo, little plates. These are cute."

As my eyes scanned the display I felt disappointment as I saw the only option for the letter T.

"Take root? That doesn't speak to me in this season. I feel like I am being uprooted."

"Buy it."

I don't often sense the Lord telling me to spend money, so when I do get that feeling, I listen. Usually I am talking Him into my vision and explaining why I should purchase something new even though I don't really need it.

"Alright. I'll buy it. But I don't see how it's fitting for where I'm at right now."

At that time "taking root" was the last thing I wanted to do. Truthfully, I just wanted to be transplanted. I wanted a new place to thrive. I wanted to be placed somewhere different where I could have a fresh start. I wanted to be removed from my current soil so that I would no longer be associated with roots that produced bad fruit.

Being in ministry and dealing with mental health issues and all that came out of that season left me wanting to run far away. As much as I loved where we were at, and as much as I felt at home in my city, I wondered if I could ever thrive again after a season of drought.

The idea of hunkering down when all I wanted was for God to dig up my roots and place them in new soil was very discouraging to me.

"I can't thrive here. I need a change."

That had become my mindset for almost a year prior to this moment. If anything, I was learning a lesson in patience and trust. It's the worst. I don't care what anyone says.

As I picked up that plate, I vividly remember thinking to myself, "He probably just wants me to have this so that when we move on I'll come back to this moment and remember to take root so I can thrive in my new season."

Take root means to become settled and established so a plant can begin to thrive and grow.

Often times we believe that means an immediate action. I am beginning to see that it's a gradual process, one that we often don't even realize is happening.

There are a lot things that have unfolded in my life over the last two years that I never would have predicted for myself or our family. Some of them I probably would have wept with discouragement if I saw the longterm picture. Others I never would have dreamed or believed would come to pass.

Lessons learned.
Answers to prayer.
God-dreams unfolding.
Huge lessons on trust.

The faithfulness of God displayed in ways I would have never known if I didn't go through some stuff.

Over a two year period of time I lived with a transplant state of mind. I was sure of outcomes that never came. I was confident I knew what would happen next, so fixated on new soil that I neglected the ground I was currently planted in.

Every day as I look at this reminder on my nightstand I am reminded of this one lesson that I have been unknowingly learning over the last few years: my job is to take root.

The plant is introduced to the soil and it takes root. It doesn't go back and forth deciding if it's really worth it. It doesn't question how long it will be there. It doesn't wonder and ask when the time will come to be transplanted.

It takes root.

It becomes established.

It fixes itself in the soil.

Take root.

Be committed to becoming established. Fix yourself on Him and where He is guiding. You never know what He is doing below the surface.

Selah

32

You Get To

It's not always in our prayers with the Creator; sometimes it is in the chair seated across from a counsellor where we find God.

"**Y**ou get to."

Those were the words of my counsellor after I boldly declared that it seemed as if most people are floating through life without a care in the world while I have to deal with all of my stuff.

"Do you really believe that?"

"Oh, yes. Yes. I most certainly do."

"Really?"

"Yes. I do. One hundred percent."

"Okay, Taigan, I am here to tell you that is simply not true. We all have stuff. Everyone. The difference is that you are dealing with yours. And you don't HAVE to—you don't have to ever think about it, or work through any of it. But you GET to."

Those words hit me the instant she spoke them over me.

I've been trying to put every situation that feels uncomfortable, annoying, or stressful through that lens.

I miss the mark a lot.
I become forgetful.
I revert back to half empty.

And then I try again.

"I don't have to, I get to."

I have the power.
I have the choice.
I have the ability to steer in the direction that I want to go.

I don't *have* to acknowledge or work on my issues or flaws: I *get* to.
I don't *have* to raise children that are well rounded and nice humans: I *get* to.
I don't *have* to stay active, and take care of my physical health: I *get* to.
I don't *have* to ever open my Bible, or say another prayer: I *get* to.
I don't *have* to get up every day and contribute to society: I *get* to.

The list could go on and on. Housework, spiritual discipline, relationship dynamics.

There are so many things that we encounter on a daily basis with a sense of dread. A feeling like we are the only ones that have to deal with it. A false narrative that tells us we are being picked on or less than because NOBODY else is dealing with any of it like we are.

My councillor told me that was simply untrue. At first I didn't believe her, but I'm starting to see that she is right.

What are you facing right now? What are you believing about your current situation? I am sure it feels like you are the only one. Maybe you feel like you are being picked on or tested.

Whether that's true or not, the reality is that no matter what you are facing, the fact that you are still facing it means you have chosen to keep looking at it head on.

You could turn away, you could run, you could make an excuse for why you don't need to tackle it. You could probably find a way to support your decision.

The truth is that you don't have to do anything. You could ignore it all and walk away. But the freedom is found in pressing forward with an "I get to" mentality.

It's not always easy. And you'll have to remind yourself over and over that this is what you are doing. But it will be worth it and you will be better for it.

You aren't the only one. We all have stuff. It just looks a little different.

Selah

33

Little Foxes

It's not always in our steadfast focus;
sometimes it is in the little distractions where we find God.

I t won't be the big things that will take you down, but rather the little things that wear at you over time.

I was reminded of this Bible verse as I became fixated on a bunch of things that don't really matter.

Distractions.
Annoyances.
Shiny things meant to take our attention.
Little foxes.

"Don't get derailed," I heard the Lord say clearly, reminding me of what He has asked me to do. *"Remember the little foxes."*

Huh? What does that have to do with anything? Does it even apply? I remembered Joyce Meyer talking about this verse when I was a teenager. It has always stuck with me.

> *"You must catch the troubling foxes, those sly little foxes that hinder our relationship. For they raid our vineyard to ruin what I've planted within you. Will you catch them and remove them for me? We will do it together."* Song of Songs 2:15

It's very easy to get off track. To forget where we are going or what we left behind for what is ahead.

It's easy to become fixated on things that don't matter but appear to hold much weight.

It's really easy to let the small, insignificant things creep in and raid what has been planted within us.

I do it all the time.

I have become increasingly aware of the vineyard that is being planted within me and the fruit that He is producing—but now I am learning about the little foxes.

What will you do to protect your growth?
What will you do to guard your heart?
What will you do to keep your peace?
What will you do to prevent them from hindering your relationship with Him?

It won't be the big things that will take you down, but rather the small, seemingly insignificant things that will wear at you over time.

This may not resonate with you—I am likely writing this for myself—but I feel compelled to remind us all about the little foxes.

Don't sit back and let them ruin what you have grown.

When those little suckers start to raid what is yours, shoo them out and protect what you are growing, with the Lord.

Where have you let the small things wear you down?
What insignificant things are you allowing to derail you?
Where have the little things begun to spoil the larger picture?

Ask the Lord to show you, and together you can catch them.

Selah

34

Good Books

It's not in our desire to be seen and our need to be heard;
it is in our ability remain silent where we find God.

"Sooner or later truth always comes around, and God keeps good books."

My mother-in-law said this to me the first year I was married, and it has stuck with me ever since.

When I was younger, I used it as a score keeper. Something I could say when I wanted to be justified or felt I was being scorned.

Now I use it as a reminder. A quiet whisper that I say under my breath when I want to set things straight, prove a point, or use it for vindication.

"That's not who you are now," God has reminded me over and over as I

have grown.

You are not the defender of your reputation. Sooner or later your fruit will show, and that is what will speak. For the good or bad.

When people speak poorly or try and twist another person's view of you, that's not your battle to fight.

> *"The Lord will fight for you, and you have only to be silent."*
> Exodus 14:14

When you know who you belong to, you can rest in assurance that He will fight for you. You don't need to say anything.

You don't need to justify.
Reason.
Explain.
Set the record straight.
Prove a point.

Sooner or later truth always comes around.

And God keeps good books.

He doesn't miss a thing.
The great judge.
The truth-teller.
Peace keeper.
Reputation builder.

Words are great revealers of the condition of the heart.

Stay still and keep silent.

Eventually things have a way of revealing themselves.

Selah

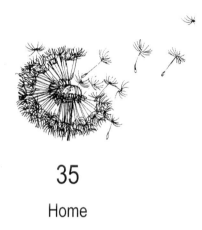

35

Home

*It's not always within the walls of a church building;
often times it is within the walls of a home where we find God.*

I attended a leadership conference in California called Catalyst. During our time there, we sat through a message and I became overwhelmed with conviction. I felt the Lord was pushing on the issue of materialism in my life. It was at this conference where I felt He was asking us to downsize, to live with what made more sense for our family at the time and less for what other people thought about us.

As we entered this season of obedience, I had a strong peace about it. It felt right. It seemed right. However, within about a week of making our move, I began to question our decision and I wondered if I had heard God at all.

Many times over the four-and-a-half years that we lived in that home, I felt that I had been cursed by God. Tricked. Teased. Laughed at. Mocked. I was convinced that I heard wrong, and over the last two years that we were there I had chalked my decision up to mental illness—anxiety that forced me to make a rash decision. "I probably just thought I heard Him. But how could I hear clearly when I was so sick?"

After a lot of prayer, and waiting for many confirmations, assurances, feelings of peace, and planning, we moved into a perfect home for us.

As I sat in my new home, a place where I have never felt more at peace, I found myself asking the Lord: "What was it all for?"

I thought that I was entering a season where I needed to learn about materialism.

Minimalism.
Shaking off the need for more.
The desire to impress.
That our identity is not in what we possess.

And I did learn all of that. But I have known for a few years that He was doing something deeper. I just didn't know what it was.

"What was it all for? It seemed quite cruel. There could have been another way."

"I was teaching you about the value of a home."

The importance of a safe place.
The priority of peace.
The joy of hospitality.
The godly desire to settle in.

For me, a house was always just a place to put my stuff and sleep in. It's why I could flippantly move—walk away, and carry on to the next place over and over again.

A house for me had always been a temporary building. Never long term. I associate homes with years not memories. I was convinced that I should never get attached, so I never settled in.

I never cared about a house becoming a home because I didn't understand the difference. In fact, when we would hang a picture or put something up (never anything personal or meaningful because that felt too long term) I would jokingly say to Matt: "There, we made this house a home."

"I was teaching you about the value of a home."

I can't keep track of how many times I have mulled that statement over in my head.

It's so real to me.

It is a salve that soothes the pain all those times that I thought I had heard wrong.

It's the assurance that it wasn't all for nothing.

It's the joy in knowing that He cares for every aspect of my life, that He would even lead me in places of darkness so I could understand the value of light.

I have only scratched the surface with this revelation. It is a conversation that is ongoing with Him as He teaches me about home.

There is so much more to take in.

All I know is that I feel the difference.

I understand why.

And I am thankful. And I dare say, I would even walk through it all again to know what I now know.

Walking in obedience doesn't always feel good. It doesn't make sense. Sometimes it doesn't look wise. Many times it will feel like two steps backward when you are supposed to be moving forward.

All I know is that you have to keep moving.

Sooner or later you will get where you are supposed to be.

He's always doing something, and someday it will all make sense.

Selah

36

Grace To Go Through

It's not in our ability to get by or get through;
it is in the grace as we go through where we find God.

"Today, whatever I need to do, just give me the grace to go through."

I found myself whispering these words one morning as I felt the dawning of a new day.

Some days there just isn't enough energy. I don't want to face all of the responsibility. The to-do list seems endless. The house never seems to stay the way I like it. The laundry is never ending. These kids always insist on eating.

I once heard a quote from one of my favourite teachers that left me thinking. He talked about the need to not let the ins and outs of life drain you to the point where you have nothing left for your family. He reminded me of the natural tendency for parents to give it all they have, and then find themselves at the end of the day with nothing left to give.

This is often a struggle for me. By the time night rolls around, I am sick of loud noises. Talking. Lights. Background noises. I just simply want to be in a dimly lit room, alone with my thoughts and a podcast.

Whether it's the end of the day, or just the beginning, some days I know what is ahead of me and I can choose the way that I want to tackle it.

Resentment.
Exhaustion.
Laziness.
Survival mode.

Today I heard Him speak so clearly.

"Whatever it is that you need to do, I will give you the grace to go through."

I haven't perfected it.
I am not a motherhood role model.
Life isn't rainbows and unicorns 24/7.

However, I felt the difference.

Baby cries.
Grace to go through.

Child grumbles about boredom.
Grace to go through.

More dishes.
Grace to go through.

Another load of laundry.
Grace to go through.

Soon resentment turns to accomplishment and exhaustion is overcome with a burst of energy.

It's a change from the inside out, and the chain reaction is undeniable.

Soon the tone of the home changes.

Joy becomes the background noise.

Peace becomes the vibe.

And grace is extended to everyone from everyone.

As I lay in my dimly lit room with no background noise but a snoring 6-year-old beside me, I found myself in an exhausted state of gratitude.

For another day.
For another lesson.
For another reminder.
For another opportunity to grow.

Whatever you need to do, there is grace to go through.

Start by telling yourself that.
Eventually you will start to believe it.
And eventually you will start to live it too.

Selah

37

Postpartum

*It's not always in the hormonal high of birthing
a new life; sometimes it is in the sobs
buried low beneath the covers where we find God.*

I will never forget the day I realized that I had a postpartum mental health issue. I still remember the way our bedroom was set up. I still remember the bedding. I still remember what I was wearing. In fact, that day—that moment—is one of the last things I remember before my life blacks out for four years.

My son was about 7 months old and the weight of motherhood was settling in. It was becoming increasingly clear that this child wasn't going anywhere and there was no turning back from motherhood. That may sound selfish to you, but for me, the weight of my new role became crushing. I was terrified, tired, and sad. I had no family support and a husband that was out constantly for his job.

At first it started with a feeling of needing a break. Then it turned into wishing I could just sleep for ten minutes, to rest. And then it turned to wanting to sleep and retreat from the world—daily… hourly… and then constantly.

I remember crying, and as the hot tears rolled down my face, saying out loud: "I can't do this! What did I get myself into?"

There are some things you cannot prepare a new mom for. As much as you want to prepare them for motherhood, there are some things they won't understand until they experience it for themselves. It's almost like raising a child: wishing you could prepare them and lighten their journey, but knowing that living it out is likely the only way they will learn for themselves.

As much as people tried to tell me about motherhood when I was pregnant, there was only so much they could prepare me for. The rest I had to experience for myself.

Instead of being told the negative or daunting aspects of motherhood, I have made it my goal when talking to expectant moms to share with them my list of realistic expectations.

Instead of telling them what motherhood will be like, with definitive answers and ideals, I give a list of things they may experience or feel and I remind them that when the guilt sets in, the feelings they are experiencing are normal.

In our social-media-centred and influencer-filled world there is so much glamour and filtered-out aspects of motherhood. From the moment we find out we are expecting, it becomes a big production. First it is the announcement: make sure it is creative and never been done before. Then comes the gender reveal: find a new and exciting way to share that with the world. It's the 'bump shots' and expectations to look like a fitness junkie that made just enough room to fit a baby around their abs. It's the nursery reveal (because that surely is a status symbol). Then, when you finally deliver the baby, it better have a unique-but-not-too-crazy name; make sure it's just enough for them to stand out, but not too much that they get made fun of. And what about that birth announcement? Do you have a letter board and matching outfit from Etsy ready to go?

The pre-game hype for motherhood is a lot. All of that "stuff" can be a great distraction for the actual role of motherhood. We can get so distracted by making sure we check off the list of social media standards that it creates a false sense of hype that never satisfies the approval we are looking for. Once the likes calm down and the excitement goes away, we are left with the reality that we actually have to raise this child.

Morning and night.
Day in and out.
Birth to adulthood.
Toddler to teenager.

It is overwhelming and exciting all at once. *Me?* You have entrusted *me* with this little seven pound package of perfection? *Me?* You have decided that *I* am worthy enough to take care of this little person until one day they can do it on their own?

When I think back to that young new mom, crying out from under the blankets with hot tears streaming down her face, I wish I could go back and put my arms around her.

I wish I could go back and hold her as she cried.

I wish I could tell her that everything she was feeling and experiencing was normal.

I wish I could tell her that she wasn't a bad mom; that she wasn't failing to reach the high calling of motherhood.

I wish I could tell her that yes, in fact, motherhood is hard, and we don't have to pretend that it isn't.

I have come to realize that the things I wish I could go back and say or do are not just meant to be left as regrets or wishes that will never come true. They are promptings to reach beyond myself and my experience and share them with someone who needs them now.

Since I can't go back and wrap my arms around that new mama and speak truth over her, I'm going to do it for you.

Here is the truth about motherhood:

At first you will ride high on an adrenaline shot of joy and excitement, delighted that your little one is finally here and feeling like you can take on anything. You will feel like you can conquer the world. At times you will think: "Surely exhaustion is just for the weak! It must be for those that don't love their baby as much as me!" Those feelings are normal and it's okay.

You will wonder if your nipples will fall off. Breastfeeding is hard—it's harder than it looks—and you are going to have sore breasts for a while. You are going to feel like that little womb gremlin is attached to you 24/7, and when you look over at your husband sleeping without interruption, you may feel mad. Those feelings are normal and it's okay.

You will feel exhausted. You will look around at people who are seemingly hacking this motherhood gig better than you, but here is a little insider secret: they're tired too. We all have different capacities for what we can hold and handle. There will always be people who have a higher capacity than you. The important part is that you remember it's normal to feel tired and how you handle it will look different. Those feelings are normal and it's okay.

You will wonder if you will ever be alone again. (This one especially goes out to my introverted mamas.) The reality that you will never be alone, responsible for just yourself, and able to take all the time you need to be one with your thoughts, is going to sink in. You will likely panic and then you will mourn. At some point you will feel guilty about your thought process and then you may feel resentful. Those feelings are normal and it's okay.

You will question if this was in fact the "right" time to have a baby and you'll wonder if you should have waited for a better time. You will wonder if maybe you should have waited another year or five, that you would have been better at the task before you if you had just prepped longer. Those feelings are normal and it's okay.

You will look around at other moms and feel inferior. Whether it's the way their body "bounced back" after pregnancy or the seemingly effortless way that they took on their new role, you will have moments of feeling less than. At times you will wonder if you aren't worthy of the same luck and you will feel envious. Those feelings are normal and it's okay.

Motherhood is the constant tethering between feeling exhausted and exhilarated by love. It is complicated and messy. It is humbling and hard. It is something that none of us can ever prepare for.

Although none of us have the same experiences, there is a thread that bonds us all together, and it is the realization that none of us are alone.

I don't care what you see on Instagram or what you have convinced yourself in your mind. None of us are immune, and no matter how wonderful one can make it seem, there are days when we all struggle.

We asks ourselves these questions.
We wonder if we are the only one.
We feel alone.
We doubt this role and if we are doing it justice.

While I am still early on in my motherhood journey, I am convinced that it is a double-edged sword, constantly surprising us and reminding us of who we really are.

I am often reminded of my relationship with the Lord through my own relationship with my children. Truthfully, it was motherhood that took me into a deeper understanding and relationship with Him.

Whether it is the mountaintop of childbirth, or the deep valley of postpartum depression, He isn't found solely in one or the other. He is there in both, and He is accessible to those that cry out.

I have experienced the Lord in both areas of my life, and I have always come to one conclusion: He is good.

Selah

38

None of my Business

It's not always in the opinions of others; often times it is in our ability not to care about the opinions of others where we find God.

"That's none of my business."

I am learning that this one little mindset can change everything.

What people think of me?
That's none of my business.

How people treat me?
That's none of my business.

What others are doing?
That's none of my business.

We are so immersed in a culture of knowing everything about everyone, that we believe everything is our business.

And it's not.

Especially when it starts to take a toll on our heart, our mind, and our journey.

You will never get to where you are going if you are constantly looking to see what everyone else is doing.

You will never get to where you are going if you are constantly listening to hear what everyone else is saying.

You will never get to where you are going if you are constantly becoming derailed over the opinions and words of others.

HOW PEOPLE TREAT YOU SAYS EVERYTHING ABOUT THEM AND NOTHING ABOUT YOU.

None of it is your business.

What *is* your business?

How you treat others.
How you respond to negativity.
How you guard your heart.
How you get to where you are going.
How you think about yourself.
How you treat yourself.

The list could go on, and none of it includes worrying about what other people are doing or saying.

He has shown us what is good and this is what is required of YOU:

"It's quite simple: Do what is fair and just to your neighbour, be compassionate and loyal in your love, And don't take yourself too seriously— take God seriously." Micah 6:8

The rest is none of your business.

Selah

39

Responsible

*It's not always in perfectly curated communities; often times
it is in our own pursuit of relationship where we find God.*

Any of the growth that has ever occurred in my life happened as a result of the choice to seek out a one-on-one relationship with God.

It was never because of a church, a program, or the ability to follow the religious rules.

While we like to hold on to those things and believe that they are a necessity to knowing God, the reality is that they aren't.

The personal work of knowing Him through the Word, prayer, and our history is the meat and potatoes. Church, programs, and all the other stuff that makes us feel good is the seasoning.

As I was considering my journey after a stressful morning with my daughter, the Lord reminded me of how far I have come.

The reality is that seven years ago I didn't have the tools I needed to navigate days like today.

I wasn't going to get them from other people.
I wasn't going to get them from two hours on a Sunday.
And I wasn't going to get them from behaving better.

I am only where I am today because of a personal choice to cry out to Him.

But God.

If there is anything COVID-19 can put into perspective it's this: you are responsible for your relationship with God. When the whole world shuts down, it's just you and Him.

That is terrifying if you find your identity through a community.

It is encouraging if you find yourself firmly planted on a solid foundation, built by you and Him.

I thank God for all He has done in my life. I haven't been the picture of coping perfection over the last while, but I have learned there is grace in the reality that I am human.

What would have broken me just a few years ago barely even rocks my boat now.

Where you are "at" now is not where you will always be.

Who you were then was still part of the plan.

Nothing is wasted.

He works all things together for good.

He is faithful and so trustworthy.

Those are things that you can only truly learn by going through and growing through.

Selah

40

Your Greatest Weakness

*It's not always in our areas of strength;
often times it is in our areas of weakness where we find God.*

Your areas of weakness can be an indication of your greatest strength.

A couple of years ago we attended a church planting assessment in Ontario. A few days into our assessment, we had a couples session with a registered psychologist, a counsellor, and a number of observers.

One of the observers was there to assess the assessment, to see if it would be something that their church would ever be interested in using in the future.

During this session the topic of my hypersensitivity to sound (and more specifically, our neighbours at the time) came up.

It had been a tension in our relationship for a number of years, often being the underlying cause of stress and anxiety in our home. It was the one thing that we fought about daily.

After thoroughly explaining our situation—my hypersensitivity to sounds, pain, and smells—I was sure that I was letting my crazy show. I noticed one of the silent observers staring me down.

I had been around church people long enough to know that this was going deeper. He almost launched out of his chair towards me. The psychologist glanced over at him, wondering what was happening as he spoke up: "I'm sorry. I have to say something here. I know that I am not suppose to talk but I really feel like I have to tell you something."

Oh great! I thought. *He's going to tell me to grow up, or work it out, or remind me that my crazy is showing. I know, I know. I've heard it all before.*

"I feel like you need to know that in your areas of greatest struggle you can often find your greatest strength... and the Lord wants you to know that your hypersensitivity to natural sound has been paralleled in your ability to hear the voice of the Lord speak at a heightened level in the supernatural."

That's church-speak for: your ability to be sensitive to everyday noises is also a reflection of your ability to hear the Lord when he prompts you, speaks to you, warns you, nudges you, and reveals things to you.

Tears rolled down my face with relief. I'd spent years feeling like I was a spoiled brat that didn't know how to control my temper even at the age of 33. As the kids say... I felt seen.

The man then turned to my husband and said, "You guys have to figure out what you need to do so she can have peace."

Less than three months later we were living in a new place—a place of peace—and sometimes (usually after 9 p.m.) it's so quiet I can hear myself think.

I can pause and breathe.
I can relax in peace.
I can hear the Lord speak clearer than ever before.

Don't disregard the value of that thing you find the least appealing about yourself.

Your area of weakness can be an indication of your greatest strength.

Selah

41

Here Am I

It's not always with knees bowed low at the front altar of our pretty churches; sometimes it is upright with arms held high at the foot of our messy bed where we find God.

In the fall of 2016 I found myself paralyzed between the desire to be set free from my mental illness and just accepting it for what it was.

It felt like I had carried the burden of extreme highs and lows for so long that it was just who I was.

Torn between the deep desire to speak, write, and share more about what the Lord had been doing in my life, and the voice in my head that told me I was unworthy because of the thorn in my flesh, I began to believe that my time had passed and I was surely a lost cause.

For years I so badly wanted to become a famous writer. The depths of my soul was an unending well of thoughts, feelings—and, dare I even say… opinions—many of which I thought I was meant to share so I could set others free.

"How will the Lord ever release that in my life when I'm not even free?" The thoughts would swirl around in my heart and mind on a daily basis.

A year prior, I had been reading my Bible in one of my lowest moments when the Lord spoke Isaiah 58 over my life. It was as if the words jumped off the pages and hit me in the face. I knew that change was coming.

> *"Then your light will break forth like the dawn, and your healing will quickly appear; then your righteousness[a] will go before you and the glory of the Lord will be your rear guard. Then you will call, and the Lord will answer; you will cry for help, and he will say: Here am I."* Isaiah 58:8, 9

I didn't know what it meant in that moment but something in my spirit leaped as I felt the Lord nearer than ever before. I was seen. I was heard. I was not forgotten.

A year later, after many months of worshiping at home, reading my Bible, and online church services from the comfort of my bed, the Lord delivered me from my chronic mental illness and need for medication.

It was that evening that I was watching an online church service when the speaker looked into the camera and asked for those dealing with mental illness such as "depression, anxiety, or schizophrenia" to raise their hands as an act of surrender if they wished to be healed. He then said these words: "If you are watching from home and you would like this prayed over you, stand up in your home and raise your hands."

"What's the big deal whether I stand or not?" I remember thinking to myself. "It's not like anyone will know. God knows that I want to be healed." And yet I couldn't stay laying in my bed.

In that moment it was as if I was face to face with Jesus the Healer as He asked the man at Bethesda: "Do you wish to be healed?" Who wouldn't want to be healed? It seems like a no brainer. Without a response, I metaphorically stood, took my mat, and walked as a response to His words "Get up and walk!"

I stood in my room that night, nervous and afraid that my husband would return home only to find his crazy wife weeping in our bedroom, and I prayed this simple prayer: "Jesus, heal me of my anxiety and depression."

It wasn't eloquent and well thought out. It wasn't in a tone that tried to convince Him I deserved it. It wasn't long, as if it needed to be of substance so he would even consider it.

It was short and simple and real. It was honest and raw and from the depths of my heart. It was full of faith and humility.

I didn't walk away that night with an audible voice from Heaven declaring I was healed. No, I walked away with more questions than answers.

How will I know if I am healed?
Should I keep taking my meds?
How do I respond with faith and responsibility at the same time?
What should I do next?
What does this mean?
Should I tell someone?
Should I keep asking or does that cancel out my previous faith?

It was weeks before I realized I was healed. In fact, my forgetful personality and habitual irresponsibility when it came to my medication was the only reason that I even recognized the healing.

The week that I prayed my prayer, I phoned in my refill for my medication. I had been meaning to go and pick it up multiple times throughout the week so I wouldn't miss a day when my current bottle ran out. One thing led to another, and it was a month later. I had gone weeks without taking my meds... and I was stable.

I will never forget the night I put it together. I was sitting in our basement. I jumped up off the couch and in panic and disbelief I looked around the room wide eyed, and confused.

"Have I been good lately? Like, mentally... have you noticed anything off at all?"

"No... why? I think you've actually been really great lately. Why? Taigan... Taigan...?"

Self medicating and not consistently taking my meds had been my normal for a long time. The meds would make me feel better, but then my mind would tell me that I was okay and I didn't need them anymore. I would go off of them, then I would crash, and then I would start them up again in the hopes of getting back to "normal" as quickly as possible.

"Well, it was different this time... I didn't mean to stop them. I just... I just... forgot! But I feel better than ever. And I prayed for this. Do you think? Could this be an answer to prayer...?"

Truthfully, I didn't care what his response was that night. In that moment, I knew I was healed.

This is the part of the story where people with mental illness either find hope or offence. When we are low, we want to be low with others.

"Misery loves company." Have you ever heard that phrase before? I used to love reading, meeting, or talking to others that were as miserable and jaded as I was. It made me feel vindicated and supported. It made me feel less lonely.

I would roll my eyes when I heard about good news in other people's lives. I didn't believe in healing and I questioned whether it was truly possible to be healed from something that had to do with the mind.

And yet here I am, a living story of how He delivered me from the thing that paralyzed me.

Why me? I will never know.

All I know is that if He did it for me, He can do it for you.

And maybe that's why He did for me, because He knew I would tell you what is possible for you too.

This chapter has been the stalling point of this book for the last three years. I could never bring myself to a place of writing it.

Maybe it was shame.
Maybe it was fear.
Maybe it was worry.

I didn't want to offend, or make others feel inferior.
I didn't want to brag, or scare people off.
I didn't want to jinx it.

Maybe I wanted to make sure that it was real.

While there have been moments of anxiety based on circumstances and everyday life, I can truly say that I have overcome chronic anxiety.

While there have been opportunities for me to become anxious and overthink, to be led down a road of depression, I can truly say that I have been given the tools to fight back.

Maybe you are reading this and you know all about mental illness. Maybe you are dealing with it right now. If nobody has ever told you this before, let me be the first to tell you: you can be free.

Jesus didn't die so that you could just get by. He died so that you could have life, and have it to the fullest.

That doesn't mean that it will be perfect or without troubles. Those are just part of living. It does, however, mean that you can live a good life in the midst of the trouble.

One of the great spiritual influences in my life often speaks about how he seeks out people that have experienced victory in a certain area of life, primarily areas that he is currently struggling with. Hearing their testimony, listening to them talk about how they overcame their trials, and having them pray over him, has become a spiritual warfare.

Our stories have the power to set others free because when we share what He has done for us, it reminds others of what is possible for them too.

Let me remind you of what is possible for you, as I pray a simple prayer over you:

Lord we thank you for the gift of healing. We thank you that even more than we desire freedom from the things hindering us, you desire for us to be free. We thank you for the suddenly moments where restoration occurs and we hear you speak *"Here am I!"* So Lord we ask that you set those that are dealing with anxiety, depression, or any other mental condition, free. We pray for complete healing. We pray for clear thoughts, peaceful minds, and hearts full of joy. Lord, we know that if you can do it for me, you can do it for anyone. We pray for a life that does more than just get by—but that is full, overflowing so we can share it with those all around us. We thank you for what you are going to do in the lives of each person that reads these words and prays them in their heart. In your precious and holy name, Amen.

Do you want to be healed?

He is waiting and willing.

He is here with open arms, and He says "Here am I!"

Take His hand.

Be free.

Selah

42

Go Through

*It's not always in the shortcuts and exit strategies of life;
often times it is in the going through where we find God.*

In my early 20s I used to ask God what it took to be a person that was so clearly walking close in step with Him.

I admired people with wisdom. I wanted to be as smart, deep, and close to God as them.

I wondered why God chose them to be a person of influence, and I wondered how some of those people could ever attain a relationship with the Lord that seemed unattainable.

I prayed many times to grant me the honour of being one those people. I prayed for the Lord to reveal the deepest parts of His wisdom to me. I prayed for relationship with Him that was unshakeable and full of faith.

"That sort of life is built by going through..." I felt Him whisper.

I hated that answer. I wanted the maturity without the experience.

As I ran around an indoor playground with my daughter, the Lord reminded me of how far I have come.

A long list of things to do. The knowledge that I was speaking at church the next day. The daunting task of solo parenting for the weekend. And yet, there was an absence of anxiety. There was an ability to find joy in the moment. There was a peace in knowing that my life is secure in the hands of the One who has constantly been holding me. There is so much to be thankful and joyful for.

Five years ago none of those thoughts would have even crossed my mind.

My responsibilities would have become anxiety.
My anxiety would have become anger.
My anger would have become immature outbursts.
My outbursts would become shame.
And let the cycle continue.

The lie of our lives is that we will one day "arrive" to the thing that we have been striving for, and then all will be good in our world. However, the truth is that your arrival time is constantly changing and the horizon is constantly moving because they aren't actual destinations.

The people that I grew up admiring didn't arrive to the place where I found them, in one single altar call moment. Their maturity and example was the product of many moments strung together, both the good and the bad, until their history with God looked like something I could only dream of.

They were built by going through, and He's doing the same with you.

Selah

43

Do You Trust Me?

It's not always in our ability to maintain control; often times it is in our willingness to let go where we find God.

Three years ago I started having a conversation with the Lord about wanting another baby. Bennett was in school, I was getting older, and my husband had given me a "last call" to make my decision.

I was scared.
I was afraid of sleepless nights.
I was afraid of being pregnant again.
I was afraid of breastfeeding (I hated it.)
I was afraid of toddlerhood.
I was afraid of postpartum mental health issues.
I was afraid of unknowns in my future.
I was afraid.

I had just come out of a long season of ups and downs mentally, and the Lord had delivered me from the thorn in my side: anxiety. It was only natural that I would be afraid of returning to that place again.

One night as I prayed I heard this small voice whisper: *"Do you trust me?"*

Do you trust that I am who I say that I am?
Do you trust that my intentions for you are good?
Do you trust that if it matters to you, it matters to me?
Do you trust that if I delivered you, I will see it all the way through to the other side?

He reminded me that He didn't just heal me for a moment only to return and do it all over again. He healed me and then He wrote a period next to it.

In that moment I felt free.

I took a step of faith, believing that He was who He said He was, and I left all of the fears with Him.

A year later I had my daughter.

She was a horrible sleeper.

I still hated breastfeeding, and only did it for half a year.

My husband left his job with nowhere to go.

We decided to plant a church which held so many unknowns.

Every single one of my greatest fears happened and yet life was, and has been, so peaceful.

Enjoyable.
Good.

Better than I could have expected.

In my release of control and willingness to hand it over to the Lord, He has directed, guided, provided, and carried us consistently over the last 3 years.

As I thought about 2020 this weekend, I found myself laughing out loud and saying: "I would have never survived a year like this 5 years ago."

Quicker than I could speak the words, I heard the Lord whisper: *"You made a decision to trust me with your deepest fears, and now it's a part of who you are."*

Faith is habitual.
Faith is a muscle.
Faith is one step at a time... moving forward.

My "yes" to a new life unleashed a life of faith in me.

It never surprises me when people are enamoured by my daughter or say that there is something special about her, because (almost) every time I look at her, I am reminded of the faithfulness of God.

When I see her, I see trust.
When I see her, I see freedom.
When I see her, I see promise.
When I see her, I see life.

What are you holding on to that God is asking you to hand over? I promise you that it's much more enjoyable to NOT be in control... I love being taken care of.

You may think that your fears are minimal in comparison to some, but He rewards those that are faithful with the small to be rulers over much more.

Hand over your small thing.

He's got so much more.

When I was young, I wished that I was a great hero of the faith. I was mesmerized by godly people that walked out a life of faith, and didn't just attend church.

Over the years I have come to realize that the only thing that was special about those people was their willingness to say "yes."

They trusted.
They took single steps.
They believed.
They used their history with God as a reminder each time He asked them
    to believe again.

I promise you this:

He is trustworthy.
He is faithful.
He is good.
He wants you to live—not just get by.

"Do you trust me?"

Become a person that responds with: "Yes."

Selah

44

Faith is a Miracle

It's not always in our wishing and waiting; often times it is in our willingness to learn from others where we find God.

Over the last four years I have encountered many situations and circumstances that have provided opportunities for anxiety.

Having another baby, transitioning in ministry, an unknown future, church planting, unfavourable living situations, parenting, finances, and many other situations have required that I flex my muscle of faith.

When God delivered me from chronic and crippling anxiety, it didn't mean that I would never get anxious again. Part of our human experience is that we will encounter many opportunities over our lifetime that will offer anxiety. The decision to either take them up on the offer, or dismiss them with trust, is ours.

When I write about healing, what I really want to offer is hope.

Maybe you are wondering "Why hasn't that happened to me?"

I know. That question doesn't always feel hopeful. I used to think the same thing, too.

I wondered why I wasn't good enough or high enough on God's priority list to make me better. I felt insignificant and second class in His Master plan. I felt plagued, and much like Paul, I pleaded with the Lord to remove the thorn (of mental illness) from my side.

And yet, just as He spoke to Paul, He spoke to me:

> *"My grace is sufficient for you, and my power finds its full expression through your weakness."* 2 Corinthians 12:6-10

His grace carried me, until His mercy delivered me. And when I was set free, I found myself celebrating my weaknesses and darkest hour, because it was there that I found God.

He showed up for me in the middle of my sickness.
He showed up for me in the middle of my fear.
He showed up for me in the middle of my pain.

When He showed up it wasn't just so He could remind me of my weakness, it was so that He could show me His strength.

When you are living in chaos, you don't realize it. Everything is all over the place. It's hard to know which way is up or down. It's hard to understand what is going on around you. It's hard to see anything with great clarity.

As an observer, you can be outside looking in and see that a person is being spun in many different directions; and just like an observer at the gate of a carnival ride, it can make you feel sick just watching it.

It is not our job to watch, shrug our shoulders, and walk away.
It is not our job to watch, form an opinion, and write people off.
It is not our job to watch and yell with instructions from the outside in.

It is our job to yell, "Stop the ride!" to walk through the gate and escort them off the carousel.

This is what it means to engage in prayer and testimony.

To share our stories.
To pray from a place of testimony.
To believe for others what He has done for us.

Selah

45

Offence is a Choice

It's not always in our inherited faith;
often times it is in our stubborn offence where we find God.

" It's easier to be offended than to have faith."

This is what the Lord placed on my heart when someone shared that they felt annoyed with me for claiming healing from anxiety and depression.

This is not the first time this has happened to me and it won't be the last; however, as someone living in a faith community, it always surprises me when Christians get mad about it.

"What does that say to other people that haven't been healed and are still dealing with it?"

This is the point of the conversation where I wonder if they understand the power of testimony. It also reminds me that they still see God as someone that plays favourites from the sky and not as a Father.

He isn't granting healing based on favourites or rank.

It says: "If He did it for me, He can do it for you." That will forever be my testimony in many areas of my life... how that looks varies.

"What does that say for people that have to take medication and are just fine doing it?"

They should keep taking it. There's nothing wrong with that. But I wasn't fine with it. That is what inspired me to pray.

I'm never quite sure what people want me to say. It seems everyone is looking for a reason to be offended... even to the point of being offended that God did something positive in someone else's life.

Would you feel better if I apologized and said I was sorry for being fed up with how I felt for over three years?

Would you feel better if I told you that I just decided to accept it, believing I could never experience joy again?

Would you feel better if I continued to live on, miserable, hating everyone, and experiencing paralyzingly anxiety on a daily basis?

Would you feel better if I continued to live on, so angry that it leaked out into every area of my life?

It doesn't sound like a way of life for someone who has been told from God Himself that He came so that we may *"have life, and have it to the fullest."* (John 10:10)

As Christians it often feels you are damned if you do and damned if you don't.

People want you to have faith... but not so much that it threatens theirs.

People want you to succeed... but not so much in fear you get ahead.

People want you to be healed... but nothing too crazy, in fear that we offend others that may still be experiencing the same pain.

Maybe we only want to believe the "fairy tale" stories of faith that we read about in the Bible because they are further away from our current reality.

I suppose Jesus spitting on mud and rubbing it on a blind man's eyes is more palatable to our Sunday school faith, than a 32-year-old woman praying in the privacy of her bedroom one Sunday night in 2016.

"I can't believe she would claim healing."

Believe it. I am doing it right here, right now, and I am sorry if that upsets you.

I heard a stat that said it takes between two to three years for people to believe a healing claim. People will continually look for hints that it didn't take place—both the person that experienced the healing, and the community around them. And trust me, there have been many "what if" moments for me.

If it makes you feel better, I have been praying for breakthrough and healing in another area of my life for eight years and nothing has happened yet... and I keep praying. And one day, when it does happen, you better believe I will talk about that too.

When I see another experience breakthrough in the same area I don't pout, put my hands on my hips, and grunt—"Well what does this say for ME!"—like my young daughter. No, I often say, "If He did it for them,

He can do it for me too. I believe it, Lord."

Then I remember Paul:

> *"three times I pleaded for the Lord to take it away from me... Yet He said to me 'My grace is sufficient for you.'"* Corinthians 12:8

And I remember Jesus himself, as He approached the cross:

> *"Father, if you are willing, take this cup from me..."* Luke 22:42

Yet, He still went to that tree.

That night wasn't the first night I prayed, and many times I thought I was a lost cause. Every time I prayed I thought, "Just one more time."

Let me reassure you: if I wasn't healed, and it wasn't God, 2020 would have been the year that took me down. It didn't, and I am still here claiming what I claimed four years ago.

I won't ever apologize for what I experienced in 2016 and how it dramatically changed my life for the better. I won't apologize for talking about it. I won't apologize for being a woman that was so done with living and feeling a certain way that I cried out to God.

I am sorry that I still, to this day, have people angry about it.

There is nothing I can say that will make it better for you, because when it comes to your heart towards the situation, it is one hundred percent on you.

All I can say is that it happened, it is real, it had nothing to do with me, and everything to do with Him and I will forever give Him the praise, even if it offends you.

46

I'm Not Participating in This

*It's not always in our willingness to go with the
flow; often times it is in our ability to make
our own decisions where we find God.*

Someone on my Instagram shared that they had messaged their kids' school and told them they would not be participating in online learning for their family.

I remember thinking to myself: "Huh. I didn't know you could do that."—and then I went on with my day.

I caught myself thinking about that phrase and what it means for me. Lately I've become tired of being told what to do. Mask wearing, who I can socialize with, what I can do for extracurricular activities, how many people I can have in my home. The list of regulations, protocols, and rules are endless, and although I can understand why most of them are necessary, I'm still over it.

Yet, in the midst of it all, I was reminded that there are still a number of areas in my life where I can choose to say, "I am not participating in that."

Negativity, fear, and anxiety: *I'm not participating.*
People pleasing, fear of other people's opinion of me: *I'm not participating.*
Defeat, hopelessness, and exhaustion: *I'm not participating.*
Disrespect of boundaries, over-working, and feelings of worthlessness: *I'm not participating.*

Maybe there is something sitting at the top of your brain and mind. Lingering. Hovering. Waiting for you to say: "I'm not participating."

Unlike a lot of things in our world right now, we have a choice. We have the power to take every thought captive.

> *"We capture, like prisoners of war, every thought and insist that it bow in obedience to the Anointed One."* 2 Corinthians 10:5

When we say, "I'm not participating in that," we save our energy for the things worth spending it on.

When we say, "I'm not participating in that," we leave room for life-giving thought processes.

When we say, "I'm not participating in that," we save ourselves mental anguish and begin to experience healthy thought patterns.

"I'm not participating in that."

A phrase that will not confine you, but rather, will set you free.

Selah

47

Thoughts on Death

It's not always in our day to day life;
often times it is in our ability to face death where we find God.

The idea of death has consumed my thoughts over the last year.

I never used to think about death. I thought I was invincible. Young. Lots left to live. For the longest time I forgot I was getting older. I managed to mentally freeze at 25.

I forgot... or maybe never considered... that one day I would die.

However, I have come to the realization for the first time in my life... that I am going to die one day.

It terrifies me.

The thought of closing my eyes and never opening them again.

Leaving behind this world and the people in it.

Not knowing when or how.

Realizing that every day I am one day closer.

The thought haunts me, and yes I know I am a practicing, professing, and passionate Jesus lover—and yet, I am still scared of death.

As I pondered death after finding out that another person that I have known my entire life had passed away, I prayed.

"How do I go on and live without this daunting fear?"

Moments later I heard His gentle response: *"Just like you didn't choose to be born, you cannot choose whether you will one day die. One was, and the other is, out of your control. Death is inevitable and is a byproduct of life. If you want to control anything, choose how you will live each day, until it's your last day."*

I use to think I was ungodly for even having the slightest fear about dying. *"If you believe what you say you believe, then why are you scared?"* my internal dialogue would ask.

No man knows what is on the other side of our last breath, yet our faith in something greater beyond the grave is what fuels our hope.

In all of my fear... questions... realizations... and worry, I am learning about life.

Solomon describes it as:

Short.
Meaningless.

Temporary.

Repetitive.

A chasing of something we will never catch.

And yet in the same breath He says that "wise people think about death a lot."

It is wisdom that causes us to consider the moments.

It is wisdom that causes us to put our days into perspective.

It is wisdom that causes us to see that our time is short and how we spend it matters.

It is wisdom that causes us to consider death and what it means as we live our life.

I won't be the first person to die.

And I won't be the last.

I am not the first person to be scared.

And I won't be the last.

However, instead of feeling guilty, faithless, hopeless, and ungodly, I am choosing to lean in to the questions and fears that I have.

"A wise person thinks a lot about death." Ecclesiastes 7:4

Maybe the feelings of fear are necessary so that we ask questions.

Maybe the questions are necessary so that we think.

Maybe all of the thinking is necessary so that we consider.

And maybe when we start to consider, that is when we will truly start to live.

Selah

48

Follow the Fruit

It's not always in carefully crafted words;
often times it is in the fruit where we find God.

There's an old saying I remember from my childhood: "Follow your nose!" I remember the commercials of Toucan Sam as he hunts down a bowl of Fruit Loops and then let out this phrase in a hearty tone.

Before Toucan Sam, the old saying meant this: follow your instinct and let what you are picking up on guide you to the conclusion.

I started following a church and pastor that tend to be controversial, especially for Christians that are much more holy, deep, intellectual, and definitely know "how to Christian" better than these particular people do. (eye roll)

It would upset me when people talked bad about them because I had been greatly impacted by their ministry and teaching. When I tested the teaching and not just the rumours of false narrative on the Internet, I found that it was godly. It matched up with the Bible. It was deep. It was life changing. Not because of their humanity but because of how they surrendered and allowed God to work through them.

I remember praying to God and saying, "I hate that people talk this way about them because when I look at their life I see Your hand. I am a discerning person and I see Your blessing. I see fruit in people that are godly yet real, and it sits well with me. I feel like what has been possible for them could be possible for me, and I would follow them over and over before I would follow any of the people that criticize them."

It was in that moment that the Lord whispered: *"just keep following the fruit."*

I have made it my mantra to "follow the fruit" as I navigate who I allow to speak into my life and influence me.

If there isn't much fruit, it's usually a tough sell if you want me to follow you.

If there isn't much fruit, it's usually a hard pass on allowing your influence on my life.

If there isn't much fruit, it's usually not likely that I will allow boundaries to fall so you can make your way in.

What does "follow the fruit" even mean?

It means taking advice from people that actually have signs and evidence in their life that they too have followed said advice.

It means studying others and the outcome of their decisions and deciding if I want the same. If I do, then I usually look deeper or ask questions so

I know what I need to do to experience the same.

It means looking beyond the superficial layer and seeing what the root system is like.

It means following people that have the street cred (actions) to back up their words.

I am not perfect. I don't have it all figured out. I am not better than anyone or more godly or spiritual. At best I am just a hot mess that has chosen to surrender, and I continually feel the Lord step in where I step back.

I may never be eloquent or a great leader.

I may not be politically correct or palatable to the "professionals" in the faith.

However, everyday I pray that as a follower of Jesus I produce enough good fruit that others will start to follow their nose and discover what is available for them too.

Follow the fruit.

Just like in nature, you'll know it when you see it.

"But what happens when we live God's way?

> *He brings gifts into our lives, much the same way that fruit appears in an orchard—things like affection for others, exuberance about life, serenity. We develop a willingness to stick with things, a sense of compassion in the heart, and a conviction that a basic holiness permeates things and people. We find ourselves involved in loyal commitments, not needing to force our way in life, able to marshal and direct our energies wisely."*

Galatians 5:22

49

Sometimes I Forget About God

It's not always in our streaks of perfection; often times it is in our ability to admit imperfection where we find God.

I am a Christian.
I am a person in ministry.
I am a church planter.
I am married to a pastor.
I am person that writes from the depths of my heart about God.
I am a walking testimony.

And... I still forget about God.

I still struggle with reading my Bible.
I still struggle with prayer.
I still struggle with my words.
I still struggle with my attitude.

I still struggle with my mood.
I still struggle... a lot.

I told my husband that I feel like I am drowning under the weight of the water that is my current life.

Truthfully, nothing has changed. When I consider all that has occurred over the last year, my life has not been drastically affected by the events of the world—in some cases it has improved—and yet I feel like the weight of the world is on my shoulders.

Virus fatigue.
Subconsciously taking on other people's stress.
Parenting in a pandemic.
Cold snaps with no relief.
Nothing to look forward to.
Social isolation.

The temptation and default is to withdraw, shut down, and numb myself from it all, and often times, for me, that includes my relationship with God.

> *"The Spirit of God has made me, And the breath of the Almighty gives me life, which inspires me."* Job 33:4

As soon as the words, "I feel like I am drowning..." left my mouth, I heard the voice of the Lord whisper to my heart: *"Return to the Breath of Life."*

In an instant I saw what I had been missing. I knew that I had wandered. I knew that I drifted from the only One that can sustain me.

I was reminded about the power of what we see, hear, and surround ourselves with. I had shifted my eyes, tuned out, and become lazy with my boundaries. I had become weak, and because I let my guard down, anything and everything made its way in.

I used to continue on in a slump, thinking this was just who I was and what my life was. Now I know that I have control over all of it and the current state of my heart isn't a slight, it's an opportunity to re-centre.

Thank God for His grace.
Thank God for His willingness to drop hints and reminders.
Thank God for calling us home when we are lost.

As I prayed and asked the Lord to be near, I felt the need to write. *"Tell them that you struggle too."*

Growing up, I often thought pastors and their spouses were some super spiritual rare unicorns that had it all figured out. I assumed they never struggled, had issues, or dealt with sin (LOL!) I thought they were an elite group of people, chosen by God because they could be trusted.

In the last fifteen years—and more specifically the last five—I have come to learn that the most effective leaders are the ones that are honest. The ones that remind you that you are not alone. The ones that leave you feeling seen, that leave you whispering the words, "I thought I was the only one..."

Here's what I want you to know: we are all bound to struggle. We are prone to wander, prone to get lazy, prone to forget, and yes at times, prone to ask if any of this Jesus stuff is even worth it. Chalk it up to our humanity. It always gets in the way.

I want to tell you that it is worth it. No matter how many times you fall. No matter how many times you mess up. No matter how many times you have to begin again.

Take it from me. I've had to dust myself off more than twice and every time I am reminded that He is—and this life is—one hundred percent worth it.

Let's keep going.

We can do it.
Especially with Him.

Lord, when we feel like we are drowning, remind us to return to the breath of the Almighty. Remind us of the One that gives us life and inspires us. You are the One that sustains us. You are the One that strengthens us. You are the One that invigorates us.

When we feel like something is missing, let us be found in You.

Selah

50

Is It For Me or For You?

*It's not always in having our preferences
or desires fulfilled; often times it is in fulfilling what
He desires where we find God.*

I s it for me or for You?

This has become the question that the Lord asks me over the last number of years, whenever I am approaching something in ministry.

For a lot of years I liked, required, and was attracted to church stuff that made me happy but wasn't really for Him.

Song choices.
Style.
Events.
Eloquent communicators.

Conferences.

Crowds.

If it wasn't up to my standard or taste, I wasn't interested.

And then I became a church planter with a minimal budget in a pandemic, and I was required to see church from a back-to-basics point of view.

And I was humbled.

"Is it for me or for You?"

This is the question that makes wrong things right, aligns my heart with His, and causes my pride to bow low.

That is the question that my husband and I filter our life and ministry through.

Is it for me, or Him?

A lot of the stuff that the western church has made top priority isn't for Him, it's for us. And truthfully, the older I get, the less I can stomach anything other than the most basic and simple of church services. Anything that takes the attention off Him and puts it on us is not what I am interested in.

My husband and I believe that our church and services are not about us. We can't save you. But He can.

"He has told you what is good, and what does the Lord require of you?"

Performance, production, platforms of influence, spotlights, eyes on me, preference?

No.

"To do what is right, to love mercy, and to walk humbly with your God." Micah 6:8

The key is to make sure that in everything we do He is still walking with us in our humility and hasn't gone down another path without us because we were so hell-bent on our own journey.

As we approached Easter Sunday—the "Super Bowl of the Christian faith" as my husband calls it—I often thought: "Are we doing enough? Do we need more than just a sermon? Is there something we should be doing to make it a bigger and better deal than a regular Sunday?"

"Are you doing it for you or for me?" He responds.

The gospel doesn't need me to make it more flashy or special. The basic and life-changing truth that Jesus died for YOU and rose for YOU, is enough. Anything additional is our belief that if we make it more palatable, more people will eat it up.

When you are hungry and in need the last thing you want is a gourmet cake. You want a home-cooked meal. Basic home-cooked meals don't need anything added to make them better.

The same is true with church.

Is the stuff that we do for the saved or the unsaved?

What are the people that don't know Jesus really interested in and looking for?

Substance.

If you are looking for a show when you attend our church, you won't get what you are looking for.

We have come to realize that we don't have what it takes to give you a great experience. We are merely men and women of faith that are on our own journey of learning what it is to walk humbly with our God.

That's what we can give you.

Basic.
Real.
Minimal.
Truthful.
Authentic.
Unfiltered.
Human.

This is the simple gospel, and this is all we should want.

Selah

51

I Still Believe

*It's not always in the deconstructing;
sometimes it is in the rebuilding where we find God.*

It's okay if you aren't deconstructing your faith. It seems as if that is the word of the day in the Christian community.

Deconstruction isn't what this is about because I have grace for that. I've been there, done that, and chances are that I will probably do it again because it's part of growth.

Crushing, breaking, and deconstructing are essential in making something new. Grapes to wine, *voila*!

This is for the people that aren't turning, leaving, or deconstructing: I want you to know that it's okay.

I had this pull towards guilt when I realized I had a faith that was sure and a stance that was secure. I remember saying to God, "Am I crazy? Am I the only one? Maybe there is something wrong with me…"

It seems everyone is questioning or leaving.

Labelling or broad-stroking.

Turning or deconstructing.

While it's okay to walk through all of those processes, I want you to know that it's okay if you still believe. I want you to know that I do too.

I still believe in Jesus.
I still believe in miracles.
I still believe in the church.
I still believe in hope.
I still believe in the Word.
I still believe in healing.
I still believe in prayer.
I still believe in peace.
I still believe that ninety goes further than one hundred.
I still believe that it's worth it.
I still believe that it all means something.
I still believe that there is grace for those that do not believe or aren't sure what they believe.

You don't have to feel guilty or bad for believing. Just because you aren't deconstructing or questioning doesn't mean you are less interesting, educated, or aware.

When I deconstructed my faith, I felt alone because my Christian circle didn't get it. Now, as I feel secure in my faith I feel alone again, and I often find myself afraid to admit that I still believe.

The fear of being irrelevant is daunting.

The fear of being illogical is intimidating.
The fear of having to justify is overwhelming.

I want you to know that if you aren't sure where you stand in your faith anymore or you're not sure where you ever stood, that's okay.

I also want you to know that if you are sure as ever and secure in what you believe, that's okay too.

One is not more elevated than the other and there is room for both. Perhaps even room for insight and growth when we observe and talk with one another.

I still believe and it's okay if you do too.

Selah

52

Church is Community

It's not always seated on wooden tabernacle pews;
sometimes it is on the steps of a camper where we find God.

While at our family camp weekend I missed two evening services. Both nights my daughter fell asleep minutes before the service started, leaving me sitting peacefully alone in our trailer.

I used to get annoyed when I would miss out on these sorts of things because I found my identity as a church going, Bible believing, Jesus lover in formal services and church buildings.

Since we have become church planters with no building of our own or place willing to rent to us, I have come to care less about the formality of a service or pride of a building.

My husband and I always joke that I could probably go forever without a formal church service because I truly am a self-feeder. I listen to church leaders that I actually really like on a daily basis and I listen to worship music all day. When it comes to being "fed," that's enough for me.

However, the piece I can never fill on my own is the community.

I have become more selective with whom I spend my time with. I have been unapologetically particular about my crowd. I have come to see what it means to share life with other people not just being friends with others because it makes my overly extroverted husband happy.

As I sat alone in the camper, both kids sleeping, I heard a bang on my door.

"Where's Bennett!? Where's Bennett!?" It was a group of boys looking for my son to come and play. In the time that I went and got him and brought him outside, another mom had stopped to make sure that I was okay and that the boys weren't bothering me.

As the boys ran off, we stood and talked for a few minutes, and then parted ways to get back to whatever we were previously doing. I smiled because I have come to love the "village" of people surrounding me.

The meaningful conversations at the beach.
The late night talks around a patio table.
The dinners with friends.
The trips and parties with our people.
The weekly Monday night dinners with our family.
The hundreds of Keurig pods we go through in a month as we sit with friends. (#ThanksCostco)
The coworkers that have become my life giving constant over the last 10 years.

"This is the church. This is why I haven't suffered over the last year," I whispered out loud as I sat back down in my chair.

It's why I can sit in silence with peace even though I know I am missing all of the music and words.

It is why I can move forward and look at church differently, refusing to force it to be what it has "always" been.

It is why the Lord started breaking down my ideals around services and buildings and began teaching me about people.

It is why no matter where I go or what I miss, I can have church because it is offered to me every day.

It just looks different.

Church is community.
It is people and relationship.
It is rejoicing and weeping.
It is everywhere and it cannot be contained within four walls.

Look around.
It's there.
It's may be different than you thought, but you can't miss it.

Selah

53

I've Found My Joy

(for Bennett)

*It's not always in the things that we chase; often times it is
in the things or people around us where we find God.*

I have never been one to print pictures. I take a lot of them but I never develop them.

Last fall I decided to take our family room and revamp it. By "decided" I mean I told my husband what I wanted, and he did all of the work. It took a few months, but it's finally getting there.

I bought some large frames and ordered two of my favourite pictures of my children to be printed.

I laughed to myself as I looked at their toddler faces. Both photos perfectly displayed their personalities. It's as if you can tell everything you need to know about each one of them by these pictures.

My mind wandered and I remembered.

I remembered the day I took that photo of my son. I had been in bed all day. In fact, I had called in sick to work and sent him off to daycare because I had a headache and I was depressed beyond the ability to get out of bed.

At the end of the day, joy walked in the room. He stood there smiling at me as if he had walked into the best surprise he'd ever been given.

Bennett. His name means "little blessed one."

Happy.
Set apart.
Joyful.
Content.

He has been all of those things and more.

I always think about the complexities in the journey of motherhood.

The hormones.
The weight of responsibility.
The ups and downs.
The crashes.
The changes.

It brought me to my lowest and saw me at my worst, and yet placed in my arms and standing right in front of me... was joy.

I often look back at this baby boy and wonder how he was so happy when I was so sad. It's like he knew that I needed whatever he possessed, and so he kept sharing with me until I had enough of my own.

He's still like that. I can hear him laughing to himself in his bedroom, thinking about his day even though he is suppose to be sleeping.

Joy-bringer.
Giggler.
Always wanting everyone to be okay.

"Everyone says I am the class clown, Mom. But it's just because I just want everyone to be happy."

Ugh. As much as it makes me proud, I worry that he remembers. I worry that he is reminded of a sad and angry mom. I wonder if he feels like it's his job to make everyone happy.

Then the Lord stops me.

I am reminded that he has made me better, not through fixing but by existing.

"Without him, you wouldn't be who you are today."

Without the death of self, I wouldn't have experienced the growth. Without the breaking, I wouldn't have known the restoration. Without walking through some of the deepest valleys, I wouldn't have been able to recognize when I was standing on the mountain.

I have come to know what it feels on the inside, that which he is projecting on the outside. I have come to realize that one thing can have multiple outcomes—both of which will serve a purpose.

Although the beginning was painful, the final outcome is joy.

Every time I see that photo I am reminded of the faithfulness of God.

Prophetic and just waiting for me to catch up.

I see restoration.

I see hope.

I see contentment.

I see joy.

I pray everyone that sees it hanging in our home feels the same way too. Benny, I found my joy when I found you.

Selah

54

Never the Same

It's not always in perfectly planned timelines
or predicable outcomes; sometimes it is woven throughout
the chaos of a global pandemic where we find God.

Remember the stat that said it can take up to three years following a healing claim for others to believe it is true? I originally thought that was outrageous, pessimistic, and unrealistic. Now I know that timeline is not only realistic but it is necessary too.

The first few years after the Lord removed chronic anxiety from my life, I waited for it to return. I searched for it in every stressful circumstance. I expected it to arrive after the birth of my daughter. I waited for it to return once the adrenaline highs of life wore off.

In the years between my healing and today I've had many opportunities to slip back in to those anxious and paralyzing moments. Child birth, transitioning from a church, the reality of an unknown future, church planting, parenting a toddler, a global pandemic.

I have said it numerous times over the last two years, and I still say it to this day: if anything was going to take me out and derail me from the work that has been done in my life, it would have happened during the pandemic.

As shutdowns began—schools moved to online learning, supply chains decreased, jobs on hold, churches told they could not meet—it seemed as though everything I had built for myself and come to rely on as absolutes were taken from me. The routines, stability, and consistencies of life were no longer guaranteed.

In the earliest days of the pandemic, as I sat in my home and processed the world around me, I remember thinking to myself: "My history with God tells me that even in this, I will be okay."

I instantly became aware of His faithfulness.
I suddenly was reminded of His nature.
I quickly remembered our History.
I enthusiastically claimed all of His promises.

And in that moment I knew I would be okay.

What I have come to realize over the last year is this: perhaps much of my healing wasn't solely a physical deliverance from a chronic mental condition and dependancy on medication; perhaps my healing revealed itself in the awareness of who He is and the deep understanding that He can be trusted with every aspect of my life. Even the parts I so badly want to control.

Much of my anxiety was wrapped up in my job, finances, ministry politics, my family's health, the realization that I still have to parent, and the fear of death.

That seems like a lot to worry about and I would be lying if I said that those areas didn't dominate every part of my thought life for a season of time.

When the Lord delivered me, peace washed over me. Every aspect of my life became less of a worry, and rather something to be lived. Suddenly, the idea of controlling each piece was less desirable because I knew His grip and attention to detail was more secure.

Imagine my surprise when the pandemic hit. Every single one of my greatest fears happened over night. My work was shut down. My finances were unknown. Our fresh little baby church closed. The unknown health implications of a virus circulated around the world. An introvert's worst nightmare: 24/7 lockdown at home with the entire family. It felt like some sort of sick joke. If it hadn't been something affecting the entire world, I would have thought that I was being tested by God.

I remember sitting in my bedroom in March of 2020 and thinking: "Don't go back to your old patterns. Fear and anxiety will not get you anywhere. Worrying about tomorrow will not help. All you have is today. God will take care of the rest."

In the weeks following that moment I would go back to that dialogue over and over again. Every time a new need or worry arose I would lift a prayer along with it. Soon fear was replaced with faith and worry was cancelled with trust.

I kept waiting for the crash, sure that I would fall apart and crumple at any moment; and yet, whenever I felt close to breaking, He would remind me of His truth.

In my humanity I had come to believe that control was necessary for survival, but what I have learned is that it is His control that is needed for my survival.

Over the course of the last two years I have experienced freedom, peace, and trust unlike any other season in my life. He provided above and beyond when I was worried about making ends meet. He changed my idea and vision of church for the better. He showed me the value of being home together as a family. He gave me eyes to see what it really means to view life as a vapour and the wisdom to enjoy the here and now.

He made all things work together for good and He taught me about trusting Him fully while He is working it all out.

I often look back and ask the Lord, "Did you really heal me? Or did you just teach me about Your nature which brought healing in its own way to me?"

I will never know the how. I just know that I am not the same, and I know it's because of Him.

Perhaps I wouldn't have experienced such assurance if it wasn't for the pandemic. It hasn't been easy. It hasn't been fun. It has been draining and exhausting. It has been trying and testing. And yet through it all I have come to know so much more deeply and profoundly that I have been redeemed and changed by the Lord.

I don't question my freedom.
I don't question my peace.
I don't question my trust.
I don't question my hope.

I don't question His existence, because I have met with Him face to face.

He is whispering in our problems.
He is whispering in our worries.
He is whispering in our anxieties.
He is whispering in our churches.
He is whispering in our workplaces.
He is whispering in our homes.

He is whispering in every facet of our lives, and each whisper brings us closer to discovering Him.

It's not always a loud audible voice
booming from Heaven; often times it is in
the whisper of our everyday moments where we find God.

Selah

About the Author

Taigan Bombay is a writer, dental hygienist, and church planter. She loves river walks, road trips, Saskatchewan summers, coffee, Judge Judy, the colour black, and candy.

Taigan has been married to her husband Matt for 16 years, and they have two children, Bennett and Vale.

She began writing in 2009 after a prompting from the Lord to start penciling her musings on paper so that she could understand herself on a deeper level. Shortly after, she started sharing her writing on her popular blog, Selah. People felt a strong connection to her honest and vulnerable writing style.

Taigan loves to speak publicly at women's events and conferences about her journey through motherhood as well as her walk with the Lord. She occasionally podcasts with her husband and speaks at their local church, South Point.

After growing up in Ontario, Taigan and Matt took a step of faith and moved to Saskatoon, SK in 2010. They continue to call Saskatoon home, and no longer are equipped to drive on any 400 series highway when they return to Ontario for visits. They are now Prairie people, and love to let everyone know that Saskatchewan is Canada's best kept secret.

Index of Themes

Biblical References

2. 2 Corinthians 3:18 AMP, MSG

5. 1 John 4:18 AMP

6. Jeremiah 17:9 MSG

7: Psalm 1 NIV

9. Jeremiah 29:13 NIV

14. Proverbs 23.7 AMP

15. Romans 6:4-5 MSG

19. Luke 10:41-42 AMP

20. Habakkuk 2:3 TLB

24. Matthew 16:24-26 VOICE

27. James 1:13 VOICE

28. Galatians 5:22-23 TPT

34. Song of Songs 2:15 TPT

35. Exodus 14:14 ESV

39 & 50. Micah 6:8 MSG

41. Isaiah 58:8-9 NIV

44. 2 Corinthians 12:6-10 TPT

45. John 10:10 AMP

45. 2 Corinthians 12:8 TPT

45. Luke 22:42 NIV

46. 2 Corinthians 10:5 TPT

47. Ecclesiastes 7:4 NLT

48. Galatians 5:22 MSG

49. Job 33:4 AMP

Made in United States
North Haven, CT
28 August 2022

23343097R00120